Violence, Slavery and Freedom between Hegel and Fanon

Violence, Slavery and Freedom between Hegel and Fanon

Edited by

Ulrike Kistner and Philippe Van Haute

WITS UNIVERSITY PRESS

Published in South Africa by:
Wits University Press
1 Jan Smuts Avenue
Johannesburg 2001

www.witspress.co.za

Compilation © Editors 2020
Chapters © Individual contributors 2020
Published edition © Wits University Press 2020
Cover artwork © Blessing Ngobeni, *Democratic Slave Master*, 2017. Courtesy of Blessing
Ngobeni and Everard Read.

First published 2020

http://dx.doi.org.10.18772/22020096239

978-1-77614-623-9 (Paperback)
978-1-77614-627-7 (Hardback)
978-1-77614-624-6 (Web PDF)
978-1-77614-625-3 (EPUB)
978-1-77614-626-0 (Mobi)

The publication of this volume was supported with funding from the Faculty of
Humanities, University of Pretoria.

Project manager: Alison Paulin
Copyeditor: Karen Press
Proofreader: Inga Norenius
Cover design: Hybrid Creative
Typeset in 11.5 point Crimson

Contents

Preface | Hegel/Fanon: Transpositions in Translations

Ulrike Kistner
Philippe Van Haute

Georg Wilhelm Friedrich Hegel (1770–1831) has cast a long shadow over decolonial thought which has fastened onto particular elements, concepts, figures of thought and interpretations of his lectures and more systematic works. While Hegel's lectures on the philosophy of history (Hegel [1837] 2001) in particular have had a bad press, his thinking on freedom realised through a dialectical process of attaining self-consciousness in history became formative for decolonial theorising. This divergence, previously taken up and sharpened in one way or another by Karl Marx, Jean-Paul Sartre, Simone de Beauvoir and Frantz Fanon, variously structures the reception of Hegel in Black Consciousness and Africana existentialism. It can be seen to indicate fault lines within the tectonics of Hegel's philosophical system itself, and tensions in the interpretations of his work between theo-logico-metaphysical speculation on the one hand, and inquiries into philosophical-historical and societal conditions of reason on the other. Yet these fault lines and tensions do not impinge on Hegel's reception in decolonial thought.

As if to hold Hegel's dialectics to its own precepts drawn together, decolonial thought instates his philosophy in the role of a vanishing mediator. Three elements, in particular, are brought to a convergence in the process: the much-vaunted 'master–slave dialectic' attributed to Hegel; his infamous statements on Africa and Africans in the Introduction to the *Philosophy of History*; and the structure of the dialectic, historically and politically understood. Concepts and figures of thought drawn from these sources have been productive, in turn, for describing and explaining the existential reality of being black in an antiblack world constituted by slavery, colonialism and racism (see for instance More 2017, p. 43). A particular reading of the master–slave dialectic, and Hegel's placement of Africa and Africans in World History, with Africa as the location of slavery (that is, unfreedom), are combined to explain how a historical legacy becomes ontologically and existentially constitutive in the form of 'slave consciousness', manifested in 'the colonial consciousness of the colonised' (see More 2017, pp. 43–44).

Yet there is good reason, we believe, to prise this convergence apart and interrogate the respective lineages of thought drawn from Hegel's work independently of each other, in order to examine the conditions of their convergence in new configurations and contexts. Some scholarship has been devoted to examining the concept of Africa in Hegel's philosophical scheme of World History (see for instance Bernasconi 1998, 2000); and to an interpretation of the dialectic attributed to Hegel, and applied to Stephen Bantu Biko's notion of black solidarity as the antithesis of white racism (see for instance Lamola 2016). Comparatively less attention has been given to a critical examination of the so-called master–slave dialectic. Close attention to this figure, and to its instantiations across different philosophical, historical and political contexts, is what brings the essays in this book together. Among the most famous instantiations of this dialectic is that articulated (albeit in negative form) by Frantz Fanon in his seminal text, *Black Skin, White Masks* ([1952] 1986).

The essays in this collection were initially prompted by the need to rethink the place of the relation between Hegel and Fanon in undergraduate philosophy courses taught in South Africa. The relation between Hegel and Fanon has become doubly displaced under the impact of calls for decolonisation of the curriculum – falling between Hegel's dialectics and colonial Manichaeism, and between postcolonial and decolonial theorising. This double displacement frames the essays collected in this volume.

The tension between the Manichaeism of the colonial world tending toward a frozen dialectic, and dialectical reason in praxis, is opened in Robert Bernasconi's Introduction. In chapter one, Ato Sekyi-Otu points to Fanon's idea of the Manichaeism of the colonial world as truncated dialectic. While Fanon upholds Hegel's idea of independent self-consciousness, to be attained through the lord–bondsman dialectic, as a normative horizon (albeit an elusive one), he sees it as thwarted by the relations of colonial racism.

Implicated in this thwarted dialectic is Fanon's observation, drawn out by Philippe Van Haute in chapter two, that Hegel's idea of the formative role of work (*Arbeit*) does not pertain to conditions of slavery and colonialism; instead, it is the role of violence that steps into its place. This philosophical account of the place of violence connects with the discussion of Fanon's pronouncements on violence provided by Beata Stawarska in chapter five.

The controversial role of violence in the context of a thwarted dialectic is taken up again in chapter six by Reingard Nethersole, who probes Jean-Paul Sartre's and Homi K. Bhabha's refractions of Hegel in their respective Forewords to Fanon's *The Wretched of the Earth* (Fanon [1961] 1967, 2004). Here we find an instance of the second displacement in the relation between Hegel and Fanon. Jean-Paul Sartre, reading Fanon in the context of the politics of decolonisation in the late 1950s, highlights the terms of the Hegelian dialectic (as mediated through Alexandre Kojève's Hegel lectures [Kojève (1947) 1980]), while they are attenuated if not effaced in Homi K. Bhabha's postcolonial psycho-affective reading of Fanon (Bhabha 1986).

There is, however, a counter-current that challenges the scenario painted in these terms. The essays by Philippe Van Haute (chapter two) and Ulrike Kistner (chapter three) show that the construal of the historical experience of slavery and colonialism to which Hegel's dialectic is being held is based on a questionable translation of Hegel's figures of *'Herr'* and *'Knecht'*. In French, the figures named by Hegel are translated as *'maître'* and *'esclave'*, popularly taken over into English as 'master' and 'slave'. These (mis)translations of Hegel have forged the dominant interpretation of the dialectic in decolonial theorising. The contributions in this collection show that it is only on the basis of this questionable translation that Fanon's (and to some extent also Sartre's) rebuttals of Hegel's dialectic make sense. But, as Robert Bernasconi's Introduction shows, Fanon's rebuttals do more than expose the inapplicability of the French Hegel to the historical slave. The essays collected here provide the steps to demonstrate this. Philippe Van Haute problematises Hegel's so-called master–slave relation, providing a detailed textual analysis of the chapter on 'Self-Consciousness' in Hegel's *Phenomenology of Spirit* ([1807] 1977) and its reception, through Alexandre Kojève's interpretation, by Fanon in the latter's *Black Skin, White Masks*. In chapter three, Ulrike Kistner takes up the reception of Hegel in postcolonial and decolonial theory, and analyses the contestations between Frantz Fanon and Octave Mannoni, based on their different readings of Hegel.

Reinstating Hegel's ontological structure of self-consciousness, and tracking it through its figures and their modulations in *The Phenomenology of Spirit* as Ulrike Kistner's chapter does, provides a picture different from that which concretises the relation of 'master' and 'slave' in particular social formations and political conjunctures. From the former perspective, moreover, the equation of attributions to the 'slave' of the *Phenomenology* with those to 'Africa', 'Africans' and 'Negroes' in the Introduction to the *Philosophy of History* becomes problematic. In his 'critical appraisal of Mbembe's colonial subjects' (chapter four), Josias Tembo takes on the task of differentiating Hegel's philosophical armatures imbricated, to contradictory effect, in Mbembe's account of the postcolony.

Moving along these counter-currents, the essays collected in this volume provide new perspectives on mediations in the reception of

Hegel's concepts and figures in post-Enlightenment philosophy transcontinentally. The contributions to this collection engage in close textual readings that highlight, in their interrelatedness, the entangled history of the translations, transpositions and transformations of Hegel in colonial, decolonising and postcolonial contexts.

References

Bernasconi, Robert (1998). 'Hegel at the Court of the Ashanti'. In Stuart Barnett (ed.), *Hegel after Derrida*. London: Routledge.

Bernasconi, Robert (2000). 'With what must the philosophy of world history begin? On the racial basis of Hegel's Eurocentrism'. *Nineteenth-Century Contexts: An Interdisciplinary Journal* 22(2): 171–201.

Bhabha, Homi K. (1986). 'Foreword: Remembering Fanon: Self, Psyche and the Colonial Condition'. In Frantz Fanon, *Black Skin, White Masks*. Translated by Charles Lam Markmann. London: Pluto Press.

Fanon, Frantz (1967). *The Wretched of the Earth* (1961). Translated by Constance Farrington. Harmondsworth: Penguin.

Fanon, Frantz (1986). *Black Skin, White Masks* (1952). Translated by Charles Lam Markmann. London: Pluto Press.

Fanon, Frantz (2004). *The Wretched of the Earth* (1961). Translated by Richard Philcox. New York: Grove Press.

Hegel, Georg Wilhelm Friedrich (1977). *Hegel's Phenomenology of Spirit* (1807). Translated by A.V. Miller. Oxford: Oxford University Press.

Hegel, Georg Wilhelm Friedrich (2001). *The Philosophy of History* (1837). Translated by John Sibree. Kitchener, Ontario: Batoche.

Kojève, Alexandre (1980). *Introduction to the Reading of Hegel: Lectures on the Phenomenology of Spirit* (1947). Assembled by Raymond Queneau, edited by Allan Bloom, translated by James H. Nichols Jr. Ithaca: Cornell University Press.

Lamola, M. John (2016). 'Biko, Hegel and the end of Black Consciousness: A historico-philosophical discourse on South African racism'. *Journal of Southern African Studies* 42(2): 183–94.

More, Mabogo Percy (2017). *Biko: Philosophy, Identity and Liberation*. Cape Town: HSRC Press.

Introduction | Fanon's French Hegel

Robert Bernasconi

Frantz Fanon's *Black Skin, White Masks* is the central text of what has come to be known as critical philosophy of race, where attention has tended to focus on the fifth chapter, 'The Lived Experience of the Black Person'. This chapter was originally published in *Esprit* in 1951 as a stand-alone essay, a fact that gave some legitimacy to the reading of it in isolation (Fanon 1951). But when *Black Skin, White Masks* was published in the following year, it became apparent that it was not representative of the whole work. 'The Lived Experience of the Black Person' highlights the white gaze that racialises blacks and rejects some of the backward-looking strategies promoted by the *Négritude* movement, especially those associated with Léopold Sédar Senghor, where the future is said to lie in reviving 'a black civilization unjustly ignored' (Fanon [1952] 2008, p. 201). The chapter ends in tears: 'I began to weep' ([1952] 2008, p. 119). By contrast, the final chapter of *Black Skin, White Masks*, 'In Guise of a Conclusion', while continuing the theme of refusing to find salvation in the past, draws most heavily on those parts of the book that are affirming and future-oriented. Indeed, the book's penultimate chapter, 'The Black Man and Recognition', ends by saying 'No' to contempt and indignity and a resounding 'Yes' to life, love and generosity ([1952] 2008, p. 197).

The second half of that same chapter is entitled 'The Black Man and Hegel', and it is the place where Fanon engages with the famous lord–bondsman dialectic from *The Phenomenology of Spirit* (Hegel [1807] 1977). These few pages (Fanon [1952] 2008, pp. 191–97) are the main focus of the essays by Philippe Van Haute, Ulrike Kistner and Josias Tembo in this book. The essays by Ato Sekyi-Otu and Reingard Nethersole mainly address dialectics in *The Wretched of the Earth* (Fanon [1961] 2004), while Beata Stawarska establishes the link between Fanon's first book and his last. Taken together, they form a valuable corrective to the pessimistic reading of Fanon that has come to dominate much of the current literature. But they do much more than this. They demonstrate why Fanon still holds the attention of philosophers throughout the world, both for his engagement with the dominant thinkers of his time and for the light these encounters are still able to shed on current racial issues.

One should not expect to find here a uniform view of Fanon's relation to Hegel. There is no consensus about what Hegel was attempting in his discussion of the lord–bondsman dialectic. Inevitably this has contributed to disagreement about what Fanon was attempting in response. In addition to the commentaries on Fanon's relation to Hegel referenced by the authors of this book, one could also mention the readings given by Gayatri Spivak (2014) and Lou Turner (1996). Given the variety of interpretations these few pages in *Black Skin, White Masks* have inspired, it might be useful to begin with what can be established with some certainty about Fanon's reading of Hegel.

First, as Philippe Van Haute, Ulrike Kistner and Josias Tembo all demonstrate in their chapters, Fanon does not address the historical Hegel but the Hegel who was dominating philosophical discussion in France at the time Fanon was writing his book, the so-called French Hegel, the Hegel primarily of Alexandre Kojève. Kojève's lectures during the 1930s were widely attended, and when extracts from them were published in 1947, his close commentary on the lord–bondsman dialectic served as the first chapter (Kojève [1947] 1969, pp. 3–30). For

Kojève and his French followers, however, Hegel's discussion was read not in terms of a lord and a bondsman, (which is what Hegel's words 'Herr' and 'Knecht' mean respectively, as Kistner makes clear) but about a master and a slave. Their misreading has encouraged generations of readers to attempt to make Hegel's account apply to slavery in the Americas through what Van Haute calls an 'anthropological reading'. Tembo confronts such a reading directly, by engaging with the work of Achille Mbembe. Fanon also takes as his starting point an anthropological reading, but, as Tembo proceeds to show, Fanon, unlike Mbembe, does not apply the Kojèvian account of the master–slave dialectic to the colonial situation. Indeed, Fanon's main point is the inapplicability of Hegel's discussion to the world he lived in. What preoccupied Fanon was not the question of what the historical Hegel meant, but the fact that the French Hegelians were attempting to apply to the world around them what they understood Hegel to be saying. Fanon signalled this focus clearly when, early in the section, even before turning to Hegel, he referenced 'the former slave' ([1952] 2008, p. 191). That Fanon set out to prove that the French Hegel cannot be appropriated for an understanding of the world that post-dated slavery is one of the themes uniting the authors published in this book.

This leads to a second point that emerges clearly from this book, and it arises from a major point of disagreement between Fanon and Kojève about the central role the latter gave to the slave's work in the history of freedom. In fact, Fanon's objection was not to Kojève alone, but also to Jean Hyppolite, another leading representative of the French Hegelians. Fanon did not read German and so he was reliant on Hyppolite's translation of Hegel's *Phenomenology* (Hegel [1807] 1947). He also seems to have consulted Hyppolite's major commentary on Hegel's text that had been published in 1946, *Genesis and Structure of Hegel's Phenomenology of Spirit* (Hyppolite [1946] 1974). So when Fanon writes of Hegel's slave that he 'finds the source of his liberation in his work' ([1952] 2008, p. 195 n. 8), he is also responding to Hyppolite, who understood Hegel to be saying that it was in work that the slave attained what he described as the authentic realisation of being-for-itself in being-in-itself (Hyppolite [1946] 1974, p. 176). But, as Fanon objected in a crucial footnote, this shows the inapplicability of the French Hegel to the historical slave. Work did not provide slaves with a path to liberation. It was simply what their masters wanted from them (Fanon [1952] 2008, p. 195 n. 8).

The importance of Hyppolite for Fanon's reading of Hegel can be underlined by a third point. It was in Hyppolite's *Genesis and Structure* that Fanon would have read that the thinghood before which the slave trembled was eliminated by work (Hyppolite [1946] 1974, p. 176). From the beginning of *Black Skin, White Masks* Fanon is concerned to demonstrate how in the colonial world black people are locked into their identity (Fanon [1952] 2008, pp. xii–xiv). Through the white gaze he is objectified: 'I came into this world anxious to uncover the meaning of things, my soul desirous to be at the origin of the world and here am an object among other objects' ([1952] 2008, p. 89). However, he subsequently introduces a decisive caveat: 'I ask that I be taken into account on the basis of my desire. I am not only here-now locked in thinghood' ([1952] 2008, p. 193). This is his direct response to Hegel's calling of being for the other 'consciousness in the shape of thinghood (*Dingheit*)' (Hegel [1807] 2018, p. 112 – §188). Fanon quite possibly connected that phrase with Aimé Césaire's equation 'colonization = thingification [*colonisation = chosification*]' (Césaire [1950] 2000, p. 42). It would explain not only why he is so insistent on confronting Hegel on this precise point, but also why his insistence that he cannot be reduced to a thing locked into its objectification reemerges at this point in his book. In any event, when Fanon rejects being reduced to thinghood, he does not use Kojève's spelling of thinghood as *chosité* (Kojève [1947] 1969, p. 16), but Hyppolite's spelling of it as *choséité* instead (Hegel [1807] 1947, p. 162), suggesting that his polemic on this point is driven more by his rejection of Hyppolite than of Kojève. So what does Fanon mean when he asks that he be taken into account on the basis of his desire? What is his desire?

The desire of the colonised to be recognised for their humanity is a recurrent topic in *Black Skin, White Masks*. It is especially pronounced in the fifth chapter, where the psychological effects of being rebuffed in this process are carefully documented. His discussion of this theme culminates in the chapter 'The Black Man and Recognition'. In the first section of this chapter, in what is a clear evocation of Hegel's lord–bondsman dialectic, Fanon describes how the desire of each Antillean to be recognised in their virility and independence renders them dependent on their fellow Antilleans (Fanon [1952] 2008, p. 187). The fact that they are frustrated in this process recalls the impasse Hegel describes whereby the lord finds that the bondsman, because he is dependent on him and thus of a lower status, cannot provide the recognition he wants (Hegel [1807] 2018, p. 114 – §192). One difference between the two cases is that Fanon insists that any description of the encounter between the Antilleans is radically incomplete if it does not refer to the social structure: when Martinicans compare themselves with their fellow Martinicans they do so 'under the patronage of the white man' (Fanon [1952] 2008, p. 190). In saying this he is referencing the argument proposed by Reingard Nethersole in chapter six of this book, according to which blacks had come to hate themselves through having internalised a racist culture by means of a process he calls 'cultural imposition' ([1952] 2008, p. 167). Hence it was from whites that they sought recognition of their humanity ([1952] 2008, p. 78).

At this point, readings of Fanon become more speculative. It seems that when, in the second section of the chapter, he turns directly to the discussion of Hegel, he reverses the terms of the impasse that underlies the lord–bondsman dialectic. The basis for doing so is the acknowledgement that through cultural imposition, the desire for recognition by whites is further perverted into the project of wanting to be like their masters ([1952] 2008, p. 125 n. 24). In the Introduction, Fanon expresses this by saying that 'the black man wants to be white' ([1952] 2008, p. xiii). This is immediately followed by the observation that 'the white man is desperately trying to achieve the rank of man' ([1952] 2008, p. xiii). This means that whites are not yet human and as a result, the Hegelian logic whereby the master cannot receive recognition from his slave is inverted into the 'vicious cycle' ([1952] 2008, p. xiv) whereby the former slaves cannot receive the recognition of their humanity that they are seeking from the colonisers, because the latter lack the humanity that would be necessary for self-recognition in the other to secure the other's humanity.

What comes next in Fanon's discussion is decisive for the trajectory that leads from *Black Skin, White Masks* to *The Wretched of the Earth*, and so must be followed in detail. That Fanon's proposed escape from the vicious cycle takes place in the context of his reading of Hegel is an indication of why understanding his relation to Hegel is so important. Fanon recognises that Hyppolite's focus on liberation through work stays within the perspective of the master insofar as the master is the main beneficiary of this work. Work does not give former slaves independence any more than it gave the slaves themselves independence; it does not remove the psychological dependency documented throughout *Black Skin, White Masks* that was embedded in the colonial culture, and that is reflected in the distorted desire of the former slaves to want to be like their masters ([1952] 2008, p. 195 n. 8). When Fanon writes that '[only] conflict and the risk it implies can, therefore, achieve human reality, in-itself-for-itself' ([1952] 2008, p. 193), he is correcting Hyppolite's reading of Hegel by turning from the perspective of the colonisers to that of the colonised.

Fanon demands that attention be given not to the former slave's work but to his or her 'negating activity' ('*mon activité négatrice*'), which Richard Philcox inexplicably translates as 'contradictory activity' ([1952] 2008, p. 193; Fanon 2011, p. 239). The allusion is once more to Kojève, who had written that 'all activity is negating' (Kojève [1947] 1969, p. 4). For Fanon, the destruction is part and parcel of the restructuring of the world that he advocates at earlier points in the book (Fanon [1952] 2008, p. 63). But, as with Kojève, it is not entirely negative. The fuller sense of what Fanon means by negating activity is what links him to Hegel most closely and allows him to sound like Hegel, even while turning him upside down: 'I pursue something other than life, insofar as I struggle [*lutte*] for the birth of a human world, in other words, a world of reciprocal recognitions' ([1952] 2008, p. 193, translation modified). The major difference is that Fanon locates himself within the struggle, whereas Hegel merely observes it.

Hegel and Fanon agree that the struggle, the fight, is not for life, for self-preservation, but for something higher. Fanon shows this when he paraphrases Hegel as saying that each self-consciousness 'wants to be recognized as an essential value outside of life, as transformation of subjective certainty (*Gewissheit*) into objective truth (*Wahrheit*)' ([1952] 2008, p. 192; Hegel [1807] 2018, p. 111 – §186; see Kojève [1947] 1969, p. 12). Fanon can underwrite this formulation by understanding it to say that the colonised surpass life when they risk their lives by fighting for the birth of 'a world of reciprocal recognitions' (Fanon [1952] 2008, p. 193). But whereas in Hegel's *Phenomenology of Spirit* reciprocal recognition awaits the end of chapter six and the final pages of the discussion of reconciliation, where it is identified with absolute spirit, following a journey in which consciousness has been educated by Greek ethical life (*Sittlichkeit*) and the Enlightenment (Hegel [1807] 2018, p. 388 – §671), in Fanon the entry into a human world does not involve him passing through a history from which he has been excluded. Fanon insists that unless the colonised risk their lives, they will remain locked in their identity and their psychopathology.

It is a great merit of Van Haute's reading that he emphasises the role of death in both Hegel's and Fanon's discussions. Death seems to be only a subsidiary theme in many English-language interpretations of the lord–bondsman relation. It is tempting to conclude that this is because the early editions of A.V. Miller's translation, which was the standard translation from 1978 until Terry Pinkard's translation of 2018, dropped the vital phrase (see Harris 1979). When Hegel turns from his discussion of servitude in relation to lordship to a discussion of what servitude is in and for itself, he acknowledges that servitude finds its essence in the lord, but he insists beyond this that it has implicit in it the experience of the truth of pure negativity. Miller's translation stops with the phrase 'its whole being has been seized with death' (Hegel [1807] 1977, p. 117 – §194). It thus omits the crucial point, said of the bondsman, that he 'felt the fear of death, the absolute master' (Hegel [1807] 2018, p. 115 – §194). Both Kojève ([1947] 1969, p. 23) and Hyppolite ([1946] 1974, p. 175) agree that the slave and not the master faced death.

Fanon agrees that facing death is decisive (Hegel [1807] 2018, p. 111 – §187), but for him it comes into the picture not, as in Hegel, to address how the slave became a slave, but rather to indicate how the former slave can be freed from the psychological dependency that arises through cultural imposition. Freedom from slavery is not enough if freedom comes to the slave from the outside, without a struggle. Much has been made of Fanon's observation that the slaves were freed without risking their lives, which ignores the Haitian revolution and all the slave revolts. Instead he highlights the struggle that African Americans were engaged in at that time (Fanon [1952] 2008, p. 196). The most one can say in his defence is that here, too, Fanon does not want to be backward-looking, as Senghor was. By contrast, he insists on fighting for a better, freer future, a future that bears its own value precisely because one has risked death ([1952] 2008, p. 194).

Fanon makes this point also in terms of action, and it seems that it is against the French Hegel that he shifts the focus from work to action. The affirmations of life, love and generosity with which chapter seven ends are all about establishing values through action ([1952] 2008, p. 199). Fanon's observation picks up on a comment from his previous chapter that associates the collapse of the black man's ego with his not being actional ([1952] 2008, p. 132). Beata Stawarska's chapter five in this book is especially helpful if one wants to understand this point about action because, even though she does not mention Hegel, she lays out how this conception of violent action as liberatory praxis links *Black Skin, White Masks* to *The Wretched of the Earth* and points the way to escaping the vicious cycle. Fanon does not advocate violence for its own sake, but because it is indispensable to liberation in the sense of psychological decolonialisation (Fanon [1961] 2004, p. 33). This became in *The Wretched of the Earth* the idea of violence as a cleansing force (*la violence désintoxique*) ([1961] 2004, p. 51). That is to say, violence is given a dialectical function.

There are a number of references to dialectics in *Black Skin, White Masks*, but it is only in the context of Fanon's questioning of Jean-Paul Sartre's account of the *Négritude* movement that its technical sense is uppermost ([1961] 2004, p. 111). However, this is the dialectic in the somewhat mechanical sequence of thesis, antithesis, synthesis, an account that at one time was attributed to Hegel, even if that association is now largely discredited. A more fluid, transformative sense of dialectic is evident in *The Wretched of the Earth*, but the immediate influence here is not Hegel but Jean-Paul Sartre's *Critique of Dialectical Reason* (Sartre [1960] 2004), a book, as Nethersole shows, that Fanon studied carefully (Bernasconi 2010). Stawarska in particular, and Nethersole to a lesser extent, defend dialectical readings of *The Wretched of the Earth* that are at odds with the impression left by the extract from Sekyi-Otu's *Fanon's Dialectic of Experience* (Sekyi-Otu 1996) that is included in chapter one of this book.

Sekyi-Otu highlights the moment when Fanon references Aristotelian logic. Fanon wrote: 'The zone inhabited by the colonized is not complementary to the zone inhabited by the colonizers. The two zones are opposed to each other, but not in the service of a higher unity. Ruled by a purely Aristotelian logic, they obey the principle of mutual [*réciproque*] exclusion. There is no possible conciliation. One of the terms is superfluous' (Fanon [1961] 2004, p. 4). Sekyi-Otu reads this as Fanon saying that it is Aristotle, not Hegel, who is 'the most truthful witness to the colonial context'. Certainly the problem that both Sartre and Fanon address in their late works, as Nethersole acknowledges, is that of the frozen dialectic, a dialectic in stasis ([1961] 2004, p. 237). This is reflected in the reciprocal homogeneity of the violence of the coloniser, and the counter-violence of the colonised is a prominent theme in *The Wretched of the Earth* ([1961] 2004, p. 46). But that was not the last word on the subject, and one should read, alongside Fanon's comments on the principle of reciprocal exclusion, these words that he would have read in Sartre: '*the only possible intelligibility of human relations is dialectical and … this intelligibility, in a concrete history whose true foundation is scarcity* can be manifested only as an antagonistic reciprocity' (Sartre [1960] 2004, p. 805). Coloniser and colonised may live in opposition to each other according to an Aristotelian logic, but their relation becomes intelligible only from a dialectical perspective. Eventually one of the opposed terms will prove superfluous, and it will not be the colonised because the colonisers are dependent on the colonised. Indeed, Fanon makes precisely that point when he quotes from the *Critique* Sartre's observation that the absurd temptation of the colonisers to massacre the colonised would be the destruction of colonisation (Fanon [1961] 2004, p. 43 citing Sartre [1960] 2004, p. 303). Furthermore, as Fanon makes clear, this happens in praxis: 'The colonised discovers the real and transforms it in the movement of his praxis, in the exercise of violence, in his project of liberation' (Fanon [1952] 2008, p. 21, translation modified). The relation of concrete praxis to dialectical reason is crucial here as a source of illumination as well as of transformation ([1961] 2004, p. 44).

With her intricate reading of the responses to *The Wretched of the Earth* from Sartre to Bhabha and beyond, Nethersole returns us to the question of who Fanon is for us today. With his notion of cultural imposition, Fanon recognises that, in the aftermath of the Nazi ideology and the strategies used to counter it, the locus of racism lay in culture more than in biology, with major implications for critical philosophy of race (Bernasconi 2019). He demonstrates the importance of dialectical reason based in praxis. He challenges the tendency to dwell in the past. He also challenges the tendency to want to close the book on European thought as unworthy of consideration. Fanon's pages on Hegel in *Black Skin, White Masks* have become a symbol of how it was in dialogue with the Western philosophical tradition, including Hegel, one of its more racist representatives, that he pushed his thought in new and radical directions. It is not by accident that *Black Skin, White Masks* culminates in a critical discussion of Hegel and the Kojèvian interpretation of history in the light of Hegel. The present volume is an excellent guide to that discussion.

References

Bernasconi, Robert (2010). 'Fanon's *The Wretched of the Earth* as the fulfillment of Sartre's *Critique of Dialectical Reason*'. *Sartre Studies International* 16(2): 36–46.

Bernasconi, Robert (2019). 'A most dangerous error: The Boasian myth of a knock-down argument against racism'. *Angelaki* 24(2): 92–103.

Césaire, Aimé (2000). *Discourse on Colonialism* (1950). Translated by Joan Pinkham. New York: Monthly Review Press.

Fanon, Frantz (1951). 'L'expérience vécue du noir'. *Esprit* 19(179): 657–59.

Fanon, Frantz (2004). *The Wretched of the Earth* (1961). Translated by Richard Philcox. New York: Grove Press.

Fanon, Frantz (2008). *Black Skin, White Masks* (1952). Translated by Richard Philcox. New York: Grove Press.

Fanon, Frantz (2011). *Oeuvres*. Paris: La Découverte.

Harris, H.S. (1979). 'Corrections and Revisions Made to the A.V. Miller Translation of Hegel's *Phenomenology of Spirit*', viewed 17 December 2019, https://yorkspace.library.yorku.ca/xmlui/handle/10315/2541.

Hegel, Georg Wilhelm Friedrich (1947). *La phénoménologie de l'esprit* (1807). Translated by Jean Hyppolite. Paris: Aubier.

Hegel, Georg Wilhelm Friedrich (1977). *Hegel's Phenomenology of Spirit* (1807). Translated by A.V. Miller. Oxford: Oxford University Press.

Hegel, Georg Wilhelm Friedrich (2018). *The Phenomenology of Spirit* (1807). Translated by Terry Pinkard. Cambridge: Cambridge University Press.

Hyppolite, Jean (1974). *Genesis and Structure of Hegel's Phenomenology of Spirit* (1946). Translated by Samuel Cherniak and John Heckman. Evanston: Northwestern University Press.

Kojève, Alexandre (1969). *Introduction to the Reading of Hegel: Lectures on the Phenomenology of Spirit* (1947). Assembled by Raymond Queneau, edited by Allan Bloom, translated by James H. Nichols Jr. New York: Basic Books.

Sartre, Jean-Paul (2004). *Critique of Dialectical Reason* (1960). Translated by Alan Sheridan-Smith. London: Verso.

Sekyi-Otu, Ato (1996). *Fanon's Dialectic of Experience*. Cambridge, Mass.: Harvard University Press.

Spivak, Gayatri Chakravorty (2014). 'Fanon Reading Hegel'. In Gayatri Chakravorty Spivak, *Readings*. Kolkata: Seagull Books.

Turner, Lou (1996). 'On the Difference between the Hegelian and Fanonian Dialectic of Lordship and Bondage'. In Lewis R. Gordon, T. Denean Sharpley-Whiting and Renee T. White (eds), *Fanon: A Critical Reader*. Oxford: Blackwell.

1 | Dialectics in Dispute, with Aristotle as Witness

Ato Sekyi-Otu

Pairs of opposites which are contraries are not in any way interdependent, but are contrary one to the other. The good is not spoken of
as the good of the bad, but as the contrary of the bad, nor is the white
spoken of as the white of the black, but as the contrary of the black.

— Aristotle, *Categories*

I am suspicious of dialectics.

— Friedrich Nietzsche, 'Letter to Georg Brandes'

Frantz Fanon's essay 'Concerning Violence' that opens his famous book
The Wretched of the Earth (Fanon 1991; originally published in 1961
under the title *Les damnés de la terre*) paraphrases Hegel's *Phenomenology of
Spirit* (Hegel [1807] 1977) and parodies his *Logic* (Hegel [1812–1816] 1969).
While it learns from Hegel's narrative how to honour and to suspect the
standpoint of immediate knowledge, it seems incongruously unwilling
to assent to the logico-ontological propositions that in Hegel's system
authorise this strategic solicitude and this ultimate suspicion. For it is not
only the Marxist version of dialectical reasoning which, according to the
famous formulation, the text asks to be 'slightly stretched'; it appears to
go after Hegel himself. As when the young Marx, in a hilariously sardonic response to the mystifying reconciliations of Hegel's 'allegory' of

mediation, says, 'Real extremes cannot be mediated precisely because they are real extremes. Nor do they require mediation, for they are opposed in essence. They have nothing in common, they do not need each other, they do not supplement each other' (Marx [1843] 1975a, p. 88), so Fanon's text here tells us that our most truthful witness to the colonial context, to the defining logic of the coloniser-colonised relation, is not Hegel but Aristotle: 'The zone where the colonized live is not complementary to the zone inhabited by the colonizers. The two zones are opposed, but not in the service of a higher unity. Obedient to the rules of pure Aristotelian logic, they both follow the principle of reciprocal exclusivity. No concili-ation is possible, for of the two terms, one is superfluous' (Fanon [1961] 1991, pp. 38–39, translation revised). Hegel is not directly named in this passage. Nevertheless, it is evident that the text here reenacts a debate with Hegel that goes back to 'The Negro and Hegel' in *Black Skin, White Masks* (Fanon [1952] 1967, pp. 216–22). There Fanon considers the cele-brated fable of recognition in the *Phenomenology* and questions its appli-cability to the colonial-racial system of mastery and bondage.

What is it about this paradigmatic narrative which 'The Negro and Hegel' finds alien to its universe of discourse and which will lead 'Concerning Violence' to invoke Aristotle's logic as a more apposite account of the colonial relation? Simply – and tautologically – put: the fact that Hegel's narrative is *dialectical* in its configuration of the origins, subsequent transformation and eventual outcome of the story of inter-subjectivity. The *Phenomenology* narrates a history of recognition whose governing principle, made manifest even in the relation of mastery and bondage, is *reciprocity*. Reciprocity is at once the foundational promise of human intercourse and the ironic outcome of its deformation. True, the plot structure revises Hegel's earlier account of desire presented in the fragment entitled 'Love': 'True union or love proper exists only between living beings who are alike in power and thus in one another's eyes liv-ing beings from every point of view; in no respect is either dead for the other' (Hegel [1797 or 1798] 1971, p. 304). Such a cosy consensualism is no longer sustainable by a philosophical anthropology chastened by the dismal science of Hobbes. What the *Phenomenology* will not jettison is the premise of reciprocity, now rendered antecedent and transcendent to the history of subjugation and inequality: reciprocity as the pristine promise of the human association in *all* its modulations.

So it is that at the origin of the encounter between his *dramatis personae*, Hegel places a scene of 'the pure Notion of recognition' consisting in 'the double movement of the two self-consciousnesses':

> Each sees *the other* do the same as it does; each does itself what it demands of the other, and therefore also does what it does only in so far as the other does the same. Action by one side only would be useless because what is to happen can only be brought about by both ... Each is for the other the middle term, through which each mediates itself with itself and unites with itself, and each is for itself, and for the other, an immediate being on its own account, which at the same time is such only through this mediation. They *recognize* themselves as *mutually recognizing* one another. (Hegel [1807] 1977, p. 112 – §184)

Presently, 'the process of the pure Notion of recognition' will come to 'exhibit the side of the inequality of the two, or the splitting-up of the middle term into the extremes which, as extremes, are opposed to one another, one being only *recognized*, the other only *recognizing*' ([1807] 1977, p. 112 – §184).

This is the momentous consequence of the 'life-and-death struggle' which 'the two self-conscious individuals' must undergo in order that they may 'raise the certainty of being *for themselves* to truth, both in the case of the other and in their own case' ([1807] 1977, pp. 114, 113). In a famous passage which Fanon would recall, Hegel affirms the necessity of violence for the process of individuation and self-authentication:

> And it is only through staking one's life that freedom is won; only thus is it proved that for self-consciousness its essential being is

not [just] being, not the *immediate* form in which it appears, not its submergence in the expanse of life, but rather that there is nothing present in it which could not be regarded as a vanishing moment, that it is only pure being-for-self. The individual who has not risked his life may well be recognized as a *person*, but he has not attained the truth of this recognition as an independent self-consciousness. ([1807] 1977, p. 114 – §187)

The result of this violent confrontation, however, cannot be the death of one partner and the survival of the other. The death of one participant would eliminate the possibility of recognition demanded by the other. Hegel therefore calls such an outcome 'an abstract negation, not the negation coming from consciousness, which supersedes in such a way as to preserve and maintain what is superseded, and consequently survives its own supersession' ([1807] 1977, pp. 114–15). The *dialectical* outcome of the 'trial by death', then, is not liquidation but the 'dissolution of that simple unity' that characterised the original being of self-consciousness and its encounter with another self-consciousness. And the consequence of this dissolution is that 'there is posited a pure self-consciousness, and a consciousness which is not purely for itself but for another, i.e. is a merely *immediate* consciousness, or consciousness in the form of *thinghood* … The former is lord, the other is bondsman' ([1807] 1977, p. 115 – §189).

But if domination occurs as an inexorable consequence of humanity's self-formation, Hegel insists that a radically dualistic mode of difference – one in which the two agents are not only unequal but 'exist as two opposed shapes of consciousness' – cannot be sustained: 'But for recognition proper the moment is lacking, that what the lord does to the other he also does to himself, and what the bondsman does to himself *he* should also do to the other. The outcome is a recognition that is one-sided and unequal' ([1807] 1977, p. 116 – §191). The offended god of reciprocity must now be avenged, but not through a simple restoration of the erstwhile relation of complementarity, a simple return to the 'pure Notion of recognition'. Rather, the act of expiation and restitution will take the form of an ironic transformation of roles.

For one thing, the victorious master confronts an 'existential impasse': he is nothing without the slave; well, not much.

> In this recognition the unessential consciousness is for the lord the object, which constitutes the *truth* of his certainty of himself. But it is clear that this object does not correspond to its Notion, but rather the object in which the lord has achieved his lordship has in reality turned out to be something quite different from an independent consciousness. What now really confronts him is not an independent consciousness, but a dependent one. He is, there-fore, not certain of *being-for-self* as truth of himself. On the con-trary, his truth is in reality the unessential consciousness and its unessential action. ([1807] 1977, pp. 116–17 – §192)

Nor is this all. The bondsman undergoes a reformation by virtue of his servile work. Was it not due to the fear of death and the love of life, mere life, that the slave succumbed to the master in the struggle for recognition? Now vanquished, he is compelled to work for the master. But in so doing the slave 'rids himself of his attachment to natural exis-tence in every single detail; and gets rid of it by working on it' ([1807] 1977, p. 117 – §194). Whereas the idle master consumes what he has not produced, the slave fashions with his labour something enduring, accomplishing thereby a surreptitious triumph over death: indepen-dence lost and regained. The product of the slave's 'formative activity' becomes irrefutable testimony to his autonomy. 'Through this redis-covery of himself by himself, the bondsman realizes that it is precisely in his work wherein he seemed to have only an alienated existence that he acquires a mind of his own' ([1807] 1977, p. 119 – §196). The tran-scendence of mere natural existence and the consciousness of freedom are no longer the special prerogative of the idle master but a human universal predicated on the norm of intersubjective reciprocity.

'The Negro and Hegel' underscores the telic primacy of the norm of reciprocity in Hegel's paradigmatic fable of recognition: 'At the foundation of Hegelian dialectic there is an absolute reciprocity which must be emphasized' (Fanon [1952] 1967, p. 217). 'Absolute reciprocity': this is the condition of possibility of the surreptitious solidarity which binds the two protagonists in peace and in war, of the inadvertent reversal of roles they undergo in the aftermath of the trial by death, and of the ironic independence which the bondsman achieves by virtue of his work. And it is precisely this founding principle and its dialectical consequences which, according to Fanon, are conspicuous by their primordial absence in the colonial-racial system of domination. Neither in the primal encounter of our two collective subjects, nor in the subsequent history of antagonism, nor in the work of the subjugated does Fanon's text detect any immanent redemptive possibilities. We are in an entirely different universe of discourse.

> I hope I have shown that here the master differs basically from the master described by Hegel. For Hegel there is reciprocity; here the master laughs at the consciousness of the slave. What he wants from the slave is not recognition but work.
>
> In the same way, the slave here is in no way identifiable with the slave who loses himself in the object and finds in his work the source of his liberation.
>
> The Negro wants to be like the master.
>
> Therefore he is less independent than the Hegelian slave.
>
> In Hegel the slave turns away from the master and turns toward the object.
>
> Here the slave turns toward the master and abandons the object. (Fanon [1952] 1967, pp. 220–21)

In a wilful misreading of the history of resistance and insurrection under plantation slavery, Fanon's text reduces the condition of the black subject to one of enforced passivity. The will to violence is here tamed by the unilateral action of the master. 'There is not an open conflict,' writes Fanon, 'between white and black. One day the White Master, *without conflict*, recognized the Negro slave' ([1952] 1967, p. 217). Again: 'Historically, the Negro steeped in the inessentiality of servitude was set free by his master. He did not fight for his freedom' ([1952] 1967, p. 219). An emancipation proclamation suddenly promoted 'the machine-animal-man to the supreme rank of *men*'. The consequence?

> The upheaval reached the Negroes from without. The black was acted upon. Values that had not been created by his actions, values that had not been born of the systolic tide of his blood, danced in a hued whirl round him. The upheaval did not make a difference. He went from one way of life to another, but not from one life to another ... The former slave, who can find in his memory no trace of the struggle for liberty or of that anguish of liberty of which Kierkegaard speaks, sits unmoved before the young white man singing and dancing on the tightrope of existence. ([1952] 1967, pp. 220–21)

That the emancipation was solely the master's deed simply reiterates the monological character of action in the black-white encounter. Not Hegel's bondsman but Nietzsche's slave is the prototype of the black subject.

Curiously, Fanon's interpreters have viewed this portrait as either a faithful successor version or an impoverished copy of the Hegelian archetype. In a suggestive attempt to show the continuing relevance of Hegel's teaching, Trent Schroyer – basing his reading more on *The Wretched of the Earth* than on *Black Skin, White Masks* – describes Fanon's analysis as a contemporary restatement of Hegel's 'sociocultural interpretation of lordship and bondage' (Schroyer 1973, pp. 96–97). On the other hand, Renate Zahar argues that 'colonialist domination and enslavement', the subject of Fanon's narrative, 'are a new historical form of the relationship between master and slave analyzed by Hegel' (Zahar

1970, pp. 86–87). Only, Fanon leaves out of his account 'the element in the Hegelian theory which alone makes the emancipation of the slave possible, namely the process of material labor', replacing it with 'the political process of emancipation through violence' (1970, pp. 86–87). In this view, Fanon ignores 'the economic derivation' of colonial alienation (1970, p. 29 n. 25). By contrast, Irene Gendzier recognises in Fanon's account the category of work. Yet this is not the redemptive work of Hegel's bondsman, but the wholly abject labour of the servant. Fanon, according to this thesis, 'may have been reflecting on the utter disdain in which the white master held the black servant, a disdain so totally destructive that it seemed to obviate any consideration of the servant, save as a labor producing machine' (Gendzier 1973, p. 26). Gendzier muses that this is the result of the 'non-philosophic sense' in which Fanon understood the category of Labour (1973, p. 26).

But this is not unlike shooting the messenger! A normative but frustrated Hegelian Marxist in many aspects of his implicit social ontology, Fanon quite evidently subscribed to the view of value attributes which that tradition ascribes to human work, even the work of the bondsman. This much is attested by Fanon's reference to the Hegelian slave 'who loses himself in the object and finds in his work the source of his liberation'. But it is precisely this normative Left-Hegelianism that leads him to discern in the drama of labour and interaction under conditions of racial bondage an entirely different, indeed heterogeneous, story. A loyal revisionist, Fanon suggests that an experience of labour disjoined from the pristine promise of reciprocal recognition is incapable of engendering the possibility of liberation. There is something far worse here, Fanon's text suggests, than the alienation of labour dramatised by Marx in the *Economic and Philosophic Manuscripts of 1844*. There the prospect of human self-realisation and emancipation through work is perverted under capitalist relations of production. 'Under these economic conditions this realisation of labour appears as *loss of realisation* for the workers; objectification as *loss of the object and bondage to it*' (Marx, [1844] 1975b, p. 272). Call it a *deformed dialectic*. 'Here,' Fanon writes contrastively of his universe of discourse, 'the slave turns toward the master and *abandons the object*.' A catachresis might best name this story of labour and interaction: *aborted dialectic*.

Nothing, in this view, redeems the 'inessentiality' of the racially subjugated by virtue of an *immanent necessity*. That is why their liberation will have to take a form altogether different from that of Hegel's slave. The story of Hegel's bondsman ends with a *refiguration* of his existential vocation. In contrast to this reformism, the emancipation of the racially subjugated will have to be nothing less than a *transfiguration* – a radical leap 'from one life to another'. Construing the colonial condition on the model of the abject captivity to which the plantation slave was allegedly condemned, 'Concerning Violence' sees in decolonisation an epiphany, a portentous event in the history of 'being':

> Decolonization never takes place unnoticed for *it has an effect on being* [*elle porte sur l'être*], it changes being fundamentally. It transforms spectators crushed with their inessentiality into privileged actors, caught in a spectacular manner by the floodlights of History. It introduces into being a peculiar rhythm, heralded by new people, a new language, a new humanity. Decolonization is a veritable creation of new human beings. But this creation owes nothing of its legitimacy to any supernatural power: the colonized 'thing' becomes human during the same process by which it frees itself. (Fanon [1961] 1991, pp. 36–37, emphasis added)

Nothing could contrast more starkly with the story of liberation which Hegel's dialectic enables the *Phenomenology* to tell than this image of the radical regeneration of 'being'. It is tempting, for this reason, to see Fanon's portrait of the coloniser-colonised relation as derived from the dismal theory of human interaction set forth by Jean-Paul Sartre in *Being and Nothingness* and the *Critique of Dialectical Reason* (Sartre [1943] 1969, [1960] 1978). It would seem that Fanon's rhetoric of 'the violence which has ruled over the ordering of the colonial world' (Fanon [1961]

1991, p. 40) is but a more sanguinary restatement of Sartre's account of human intercourse, or, worse, an endorsement of Sartre's 'phenomenology of social violence' perverted, according to William Leon McBride, into a 'romantic glorification of violence for its own sake' (McBride 1969, pp. 290–313, 321).

But if the strategic reading of 'The Negro and Hegel' and 'Concerning Violence' I have offered above is at all plausible, then both texts would seem to suggest that not only Hegel's narrative but successor narratives of social being predicated on relations of reciprocity, benign or malignant, are incapable of capturing 'the originality of the colonial context' (Fanon [1961] 1991, p. 40). Sartre's narrative, likewise, is incapable of this.

It may be recalled that in *Being and Nothingness* Sartre declares Hegel's solution to the problem of 'the existence of others' to be unsatisfactory. He is concerned to 'marshal against Hegel a twofold charge of optimism': an 'epistemological optimism' and an 'ontological optimism' parallel to it (Sartre [1943] 1969, pp. 327–28). Sartre will have nothing to do with the dialectical teleology which requires that the struggle for human recognition should terminate in a mutual disclosure, by self and other, of universal value and objective truth, an intersubjectivity of knowledge and action. Sartre asserts in response to Hegel that '[no] universal knowledge can be derived from the relations of consciousnesses. This is what we call their ontological separation' ([1943] 1969, pp. 328–29). Hegel's was but a futile project of covering 'the scandal of the plurality of consciousness' with a 'logical or epistemological optimism', an attempt to realise a 'totalitarian and unifying synthesis of "Others"' ([1943] 1969, pp. 329, 339).

For Sartre, there is no ontologically primary experience of a 'we-subject', since it is the inalienable vocation of each human being, each consciousness, to seek to transcend (the freedom of) another human being: 'We should hope in vain for a human "we" in which the intersubjective totality would obtain consciousness of itself as a unified subjectivity' (Sartre [1943] 1969, p. 553). Far from being a fundamental structure of 'human reality', such an intersubjectivity is but a fleeting 'psychological experience realized by an historic man'. The Heideggerian category of the 'Mitsein' ('Being-with') is, according to Sartre, no more ontologically predicative of human reality than the Hegelian concept of reciprocal recognition. Coexistence is not, as Heidegger supposed, 'equiprimordial with Being-in-the-world' (Heidegger [1927] 1962, p. 149). For Sartre the 'essence of the relations between consciousnesses is not the Mitsein; it is conflict' (Sartre [1943] 1969, p. 555).

Sartre's universe is a Hobbesian universe. Yet, more precisely, for this very reason, the principle of reciprocity is *not* banished from it. But reciprocity here constitutes a 'negative relation' between human beings, condemning them to a 'detotalized totality' of experience. To be sure, an egalitarian structure of intersubjectivity is a chimerical ideal: 'we shall never place ourselves concretely on a plane of equality; that is, on the plane where the recognition of the Other's freedom would involve the Other's recognition of our freedom' (Sartre [1943] 1969, pp. 339, 529). But there is available here a dreadful equality of mutual sabotage, frustration, domination and violence remarkably reminiscent of the equality of insecurity and terror which Hobbes adduced as the justification for a self-perpetuating sovereign. In his own perverse manner of standing Hegel on his head, Sartre retains an essential feature of the Hegelian paradigm of human interaction: the possibility of a mutual exchange of roles among the participants. If human beings are incapable of ever recognising one another as subjects bound together by relations of complementarity, they have an equal capacity, albeit doomed to mutual frustration, for attempting to transform one another into *objects*. It is because human beings possess this demonic power equally and are capable of deploying it reciprocally that Sartre considers the danger of domination, alienation and reification to be not a 'historical result' or an accident which is 'capable of being surmounted' but rather 'the permanent structure' of human interaction ([1943] 1969, p. 358). Human intercourse is a cyclical experience of mastery and bondage: no one has an enduring privilege of lordship; no one is condemned to a perpetual burden of servitude.

Sartre's dramatic archetype for this circle of autonomy and heteronomy, this ceaseless alteration of triumphant subjectivity and the shame of reification, is the famous phenomenon of the 'Look' ([1943] 1969, pp. 340–400). Caught in the act by the piercing look of the other, I experience an assault upon my liberty which was constitutionally sovereign in its projects and possibilities. I am endowed with a character, a nature, with objectivity. Suddenly, from being that restless lack of being, that prodigious nothingness which is the ontological structure of the *for-itself*, suddenly, writes Sartre, 'I *am* somebody'. My human reality is henceforth robbed of its protean possibilities; it is now a 'degraded, fixed, dependent being'. This 'objectivation' of my being is therefore the occasion for 'a radical metamorphosis' in the primordial structure of human reality ([1943] 1969, pp. 353, 384, 365). It is, nevertheless, a reversible experience. What is the basis for this reversibility?

It is the ontological structure of the for-itself which secures the possibility for undoing the domination and reification inflicted by the existence of others. For it is the unimpaired prerogative of the for-itself to 'assume', hence to refuse, its degradation into 'objectness'. Hegel said of the process of human recognition that 'action from one side only would be useless, because what is to happen can only be brought about by means of both' (Hegel [1807] 1977, p. 112); and Sartre's phenomenology of reification and its transcendence is reminiscent of Hegel's theory – and consistent with his own fundamental ontology. Thus, he holds that the negation of my freedom or transcendence by the other is reciprocated by a 'second negation, the one which proceeds from me' (Sartre [1943] 1969, p. 382). In short, I can in my turn look at the other, make an object out of him, and put *his* possibilities out of play. Sartre has dismissed Hegel's dialectic of reciprocity as totalitarian; he has vetoed the 'epistemological optimism' which dreams of an experiential totality shared by the ego and the other; but he has, upon the foundations of his own ontology, proposed a *negative dialectic of reciprocity* which requires that the 'dependent consciousness' be capable of transcending its reduction to the status of a thing by exchanging roles with the 'independent consciousness' (Hegel [1807] 1977, p. 117). Sartre's account of 'concrete relations with others' (Sartre [1943] 1969, pp. 471–558), his evocation of the tragicomedies of love, hate, masochism and sadism, is an elaboration of this eternal dance of involuntary freedom and willed servitude which is, according to him, the inalienable mark of the human condition.

Of this irreducible role of reciprocity in human transactions the *Critique of Dialectical Reason* is a monumental orchestration. In a renewed debate with Hegel, Sartre is concerned to exhibit 'the disquiet of reciprocity' (Sartre [1960] 1978, p. 116), not its disappearance; and to make it abundantly clear, if any doubt still remained, that 'reciprocity, though completely opposed to alienation and reification, does not save men from them' ([1960] 1978, p. 111). In short, he wants to insist that reciprocity should not be confused with perpetual peace. The hidden Kantianism of Hegel's doctrine of mutual recognition must be refused: 'We must not suppose that we have entered the kingdom of ends and that, in reciprocity, everyone recognizes and treats the Other as an absolute end' ([1960] 1978, p. 112). In this view, there is no transcendental standard of 'pure reciprocity' of which the relationship of mastery and bondage constitutes a tragic manifestation. And Sartre would invoke the idea of 'pure reciprocity' only with a sardonic intent – that is to say, in order to demonstrate its historical and ontological conditions of impossibility. More precisely, his historical explanation of 'the impossibility of coexistence' owes its 'dialectical intelligibility' to atemporal ontological postulates ([1960] 1978, p. 128). The principal terms of the ontological argument deployed by the *Critique* are practically lifted from *Being and Nothingness*. Now as before, the defining properties of the human condition are those of 'need', 'lack', 'lacuna', 'negation' (Sartre [1960] 1978, pp. 80–100, [1943] 1969, pp. 272ff.).

There is, however, a novel category that would seem to introduce the place of contingency and impermanence into these grim constancies of the human situation. And that category is *scarcity*. Sartre's version of scarcity, it turns out, is as invariable as that of his Hobbesian and liberal precursors. A being in need (*l'homme de besoin*) interacts with another being in need in a harsh world of scarcity. Sartre declares emphatically: '*There is not enough for everybody*' ([1960] 1978, pp. 127–28). Consequently, human beings are condemned to know the norm of reciprocity only in its pathological form: 'In pure reciprocity, that which is Other than me is *also the same*. But in reciprocity as *modified by scarcity*, the same appears to us as anti-human in so far as *this same man* appears as radically Other – that is to say, as threatening us with death' ([1960] 1978, pp. 131–32). Under the sway of dire necessity, each person confronts the other as belonging to '*another species*', which is to say as 'our demonic double'; for 'it is impossible for *all* those bound by reciprocal links to stay on the soil which supports and feeds them' ([1960] 1978, p. 132). The action of each person must be aimed at undoing the action and freedom of the other. 'Interiorised scarcity' is therefore 'the basic abstract matrix of every reification of human relations in any society', the material foundation for 'the constitution of radical evil and of Manichaeism' ([1960] 1978, p. 132). In a world in which every person is necessarily the 'surplus man', human intercourse is characterised by reciprocal *violence*. Far from being a degenerate condition of social existence or even a necessary means for the reconstitution of political life, violence is for Sartre nothing less than 'a structure of human action under the sway of Manichaeism and in a context of scarcity', a testimony to 'the unbearable fact of broken reciprocity and of the systematic exploitation of man's humanity for the destruction of the human' ([1960] 1978, pp. 132–33).

Manichaeism, violence, the reduction of the human being to a thing by the look and action of another human being; or the condemnation of the other to the status of a dreaded or spurned 'surplus' entity: these and other characteristic figures in Sartre's account of being-for-others reappear in Fanon's representation of the racial drama of the 'colonial context', most memorably in that lacerating evocation of the hounded consciousness, 'The Lived Experience of the Black Person [*L'expérience vécue du Noir*]', the fifth chapter of *Black Skin, White Masks*:[1] "'Dirty nigger!" Or simply, "Look, a nigger!" I came into the world imbued with the will to find a meaning in things, my spirit filled with the desire to attain to the source of the world, and then I found that I was an object in the midst of other objects' (Fanon [1952] 1967, p. 109). These words echo Sartre's characterisation of the 'radical metamorphosis' which the presence and action of the other effect in a being destined to be free: 'The for-itself when alone transcends the world; it is the nothing by which *there are* things. The Other by rising up confers on the for-itself a being-in-itself-in-the-midst-of-the-world as a thing among things' (Sartre [1943] 1969, p. 555).

But consider the interpersonal character and cyclical reciprocity of Sartre's portrait of reification, as against the intercollectivity and the norm of irreciprocity that define Fanon's schema. It may be retorted that Sartre's phenomenology is cognisant of a collective experience of being reduced to the status of things, and that Fanon's critical analysis is eminently illustrative of the phenomenon of *'The Us-Object'* in which the look and action of a third person (*'The Third'*) precipitate the self and the other into a shared experience of shame and alienation, making of the individual 'an object in a community of objects' ([1943] 1969, pp. 537–47). Sartre indeed understands that such a collective experience of reification represents 'a still more radical alienation on the part of the for-itself since the latter is no longer compelled only to assume what it is for the Other but to assume also a totality which it is not although it forms an integral part of it'. Of those human situations 'more favourable to the upsurge of the "Us"', Sartre cites the experience of belonging to an oppressed class. To the latter, the oppressing class appears as a 'perpetual Third'. And as a result of 'the privileges of the Third', I, as a member of the oppressed class, 'experience my being-looked-at-as-a-thing-engaged-in-a-totality-of-things' ([1943] 1969, pp. 541, 545).

Yet for all its coerciveness and the monstrous depersonalisation which it signifies, the experience of the us-object is, according to Sartre, 'only a more complex modality' of being-for-others. Like the reification caused by interpersonal relations, the us-object contains a structural possibility of 'disintegration'. The 'Us', writes Sartre, 'collapses as soon as the for-itself reclaims its selfness in the face of the Third and looks at him in turn'. Not only can individual selfness be recovered, but by *assuming* a class consciousness a member of the oppressed class undertakes 'the project of freeing the whole "Us" from the object-state by transforming it into a We-Subject' ([1943] 1969, pp. 545, 546). And although Sartre would declare that the experience of the 'We-Subject', of intersubjective action, is not ontologically primary but merely a historical and psychological episode, we are still witnessing a dialectical 'project of reversal' similar to the poetic justice and immanent reversibility of interpersonal reification. It is upon the basis of this fundamental doctrine that Sartre would launch his attack on objectivist conceptions of the condition of the proletariat in the *Critique*. In *Search for a Method*, the book that prefaced the *Critique*, this attack culminated in the declaration that 'we refuse to confuse the alienated man with a thing or alienation with the physical laws governing external relations' (Sartre [1957] 1963, p. 91). Thus, it matters little that class rather than race is the principal exemplar, in this context, of the phenomenon of collective reification as Sartre understands it. Sartrean existentialism regards *all* experiences of collective reification as equally daemonic, and equally redeemable because anchored in that fundamental characteristic of the human condition which is freedom.

Alas, Fanon's account of the oppressive weight of 'the white look [*le regard blanc*]' (Fanon 1952, p. 109, 1967, p. 110, translation revised) upon the black body is not marked by this macabre optimism. For one thing, that optimism is the obverse side of a fundamental conception of the for-itself and its consequences for human relations from which Fanon, for all his considerable debts to Sartre, demurs. What Paul Ricoeur described as the 'philosophical style of no', which identifies 'human reality with negativity' (Ricoeur [1955] 1970, pp. 54–55), is explicitly repudiated by Fanon in the introduction to *Black Skin, White Masks*: 'The human being is not merely a possibility of recapture, of negation. If it is true that consciousness is the activity of transcendence, we have to see, too, that this transcendence is haunted by the problems of love and understanding. The human being is a *yes* that vibrates to cosmic harmonies' ([1952] 1967, p. 10, translation revised). Fanon is prepared to entertain the plausibility of Sartre's portraits of being-for-others as studies in the pathology of human intercourse, exemplars of 'bad faith and inauthenticity'. Where Sartre's Hobbesian creatures will require a 'radical conversion' in order to accept an ethics of mutuality, Fanon, the critic of desire corrupted by race, declares: 'Today I believe in the possibility of love; that is why I endeavour to trace its imperfections, its perversions.' To the chagrin of his future postmodernist readers, Fanon subscribes to a standard of 'authentic love – wishing for others what one postulates for oneself, when that postulation unites the permanent values of human reality' – a standard that authorises his condemnation of perverse desire ([1952] 1967, p. 41).

But as dramatists of the pathological or purveyors of the normal and the normative, Sartre and Fanon present us with different situations of desire and interaction – and consequently different ways of parting company with Hegel. It may indeed be the case that it is not Fanon's but Sartre's account of desire and interaction which exhibits an 'Aristotelian logic' of 'reciprocal exclusivity' with brutal consistency. In Sartre's world, Manichaeism is an equal-opportunity employer. Each party in the self-other relation is capable of becoming *de trop*. In the colonial context, by contrast, one term and only one term in the coloniser-colonised relation is, according to Fanon (in the passage in which he invokes Aristotle's logic), *de trop*, 'superfluous' (Fanon [1961] 1991, pp. 38–39).

What then binds Sartre, phenomenologist of *normal* violence, to Fanon, critic of *colonial* violence? Stated otherwise: what authorises Sartre's valiant anticolonialism? Is Sartre's anticolonialism, unlike Fanon's, wholly adventitious to his philosophical anthropology? Sartre's explicit reflections on the colonial condition suggest ambiguous answers to this question. His introduction to Albert Memmi's *The Colonizer and the Colonized* speaks of the 'relentless reciprocity that binds the colonizer and the colonized – his product and his fate' (Sartre cited in Memmi [1957] 1967, p. xviii). Following Memmi, Sartre appears to mean by this statement that the coloniser engenders the instrument of his own destruction. Coloniser and colonised are thus seen to be bound together by a dialectical relation similar to the Hegelian nexus of master and slave and the Marxist concept of the historical reciprocity of bourgeoisie and proletariat: 'The secret of the proletariat, Marx once said, is that it bears within it the destruction of bourgeois society. We must be grateful to Memmi for reminding us that the colonized likewise has his secret, and that we are witnessing the infamous death-struggle of colonialism' (Sartre cited in Memmi [1957] 1967, p. xxix). Can the logic of the colonial-racial system and its abolition be so readily assimilated to the discourse of class relations in Marxism? This is precisely the question posed by the passage in 'Concerning Violence' which calls for Marxist analysis to be 'slightly stretched every time we have to do with the colonial problem' (Fanon [1961] 1991, p. 40). We may wonder whether Sartre's understanding of the coloniser-colonised relation suggested by the above gloss on Memmi's text is not simply a specification, in the guise of Marxist historicism, of his general theory of conflictual reciprocity. This suspicion is confirmed by Sartre's Preface to *The Wretched of the Earth* (Sartre [1961] 1991). It is here that Sartre lauds Fanon for being the first since Engels – 'if you set aside Sorel's fascist utterances' ([1961] 1991), p. 14) – to illuminate the role of violence in history. In a curious case of a misreading that is at once sympathetic and brazenly appropriative, Sartre suggests that Fanon's account of violence is but an instantiation of 'the dialectic which liberal hypocrisy hides from you and which is as much responsible for our existence as for his' ([1961] 1991, p. 14). The dialectic, doubtless, as construed by Sartre's social ontology.[2]

And indeed this annexation of colonial history to History, hinted at in the 1961 Preface, is rather more explicitly carried out earlier in those parts of the *Critique* dealing with colonialism (Sartre [1960] 1978, pp. 714–33). Sartre has two interrelated purposes in this part of the work. First, he is determined to rescue the analysis of colonialism from vulgar Marxist socioeconomic determinism. Second, he wants to show that much as the colonial experience may appear to be an antidialectic unanchored in any identifiable human volition and responsibility, there remains, at the foundation of it all, human *praxis*. It must never be forgotten that the *practico inert* – Sartre's name for the reified form that all human actions and transactions are condemned to assume – never erases the ontological principle of human agency, albeit an agency cheated of its transparency. The tyrannising reification of the roles of coloniser and colonised is no exception to this tragic law of the dialectic ([1960] 1978, pp. 713, 734).

Sartre's critique of traditional Marxist perspectives on the colonial question is compelling. He objects to the ready-made deterministic formula which would regard the destruction of indigenous social structures and institutions as 'the necessary result of the contact between two definite societies of which one is backward (or underdeveloped), agricultural and feudal, and the other industrialized'. Such an objectivist explanation, he points out, obscures the deliberate violence employed to destroy the social and judicial systems of the colonised 'the better to rob them'; it obscures, in other words, the crucial role of human intentions ([1960] 1978, p. 717).

It may be thought that Sartre's critique is here underscoring the element of *irreciprocity* in the structure of colonial violence. Add to this his suggestive characterisation of colonial Manichaeism as one that makes of the colonised – and of the colonised alone, it would seem – the 'other than man' ([1960] 1978, p. 715), and Sartre's analysis might be interpreted as stressing the fundamental deviation of the colonial relationship from the generic patterns of human interaction as he understands them to be. We discover, however, that for all its historical specificity, the phenomenon of colonial violence is only a variation on an ontological theme. Violence, including colonial violence, is still for Sartre an expression of inalienable freedom: 'The only violence conceivable is that of freedom against freedom through the mediation of inorganic matter' ([1960] 1978, p. 736). In his anxiety to extricate the analysis of colonialism from the reductionism of vulgar Marxist theory and thus to develop a *critique* of the colonial experience, Sartre ends up forcing that experience into the conceptual framework of his own Hobbesian anthropology. The commitment to anthropological universals has repressed Sartre's own intimation of the difference which the colonial world makes. Violence emerges once more as a trans-historical constant neither specific to nor definitive of the colonial experience.

Is it possible to subject the colonial order to critical judgement on the basis of this 'structural anthropology'? Can a phenomenological ontology of 'radical evil' ask in what peculiar ways the colonial condition is radically dehumanising, lacking in the minimal requirements of human association? And can it coherently generate a justification of anticolonial revolution? It would seem to be difficult to answer these questions affirmatively on the strength of Sartre's analysis in *Being and Nothingness* and the *Critique of Dialectical Reason*. To what, then, does Sartre's noble hatred of racial and colonial domination owe what might be called its contingent foundation?

There exists one clue contained in an essay that predates Sartre's pronouncements on the colonial question which I have just reviewed. The dramatic opening lines of Sartre's *Black Orpheus* (Sartre [1948] 1951) constitute, ironically, the most eloquent questioning of every future existentialist interpretation of the colonial experience – including Sartre's! In the anthology of poetic writings to which this celebrated essay was a preface (Senghor 1948), Sartre would discern a revolutionary event of cosmic significance. And the reason, Sartre tells Europe, is this:

> Here, in this anthology, are black men standing, black men who examine us; and I want you to feel, as I, the sensation of being seen. For the white man has enjoyed for three thousand years the privilege of seeing without being seen. It was a seeing pure and uncomplicated; the light of his eyes drew all things from their primeval darkness. The whiteness of his skin was a further aspect of vision, a light condensed. The white man, white because he was

man, white like the day, white as truth is white, white like virtue, lighted like a torch all creation; he unfolded the essence, secret and white, of existence. Today, the black men have fixed their gaze upon us and our gaze is thrown back in our eyes; black torches, in their turn, light the world and our white heads are only small lanterns balanced in the wind. (Sartre [1948] 1951, pp. 7–8)

The African gaze as a psychoexistential event of world-historical moment: we will appreciate the contextual truth of Sartre's lyricism if we consider its informing understanding of the imperialist epoch and the colonial relation in the light of his fundamental existential analysis of the 'Look'. The 'privilege of seeing without being seen': this impossible will to be 'pure subject' free from the asphyxiating look of the other had been identified in *Being and Nothingness* as no more than an ephemeral prerogative of every human being in his or her encounter with the other (Sartre [1943] 1969, p. 384). It was a delusional dream, thanks to the mutual alternation of the experiences of being a subject and of being an object. We are faced, in this view, with a veritable monstrosity in the shape of the colonial relation and the politics of race: the monopolistic proprietorship by the coloniser and the coloniser alone of the privilege of being 'pure subject' – a political economy of subjectivity that has no equivalent in the normal commerce of humanity. This is what the author of 'The Lived Experience of the Black Person' means when, invoking Sartre against Sartre, he declares that 'between the white person and me there is irremediably a relation of transcendence' (Fanon [1952] 1967, p. 138, translation revised). In a footnote Fanon adds the following observation: 'Though Sartre's speculations on the existence of the Other may be correct (to the extent, we must remember, to which *Being and Nothingness* describes an alienated consciousness), their application to a black consciousness proves fallacious. That is because the white man is not only the Other but also the master whether real or imaginary' ([1952] 1967, p. 138, n. 24, translation revised).

Here, then, is a drama of human(!) encounter and interaction in which no norm of reciprocity, not even a negative dialectic of murderous reciprocity, appears to prevail. *Black Skin, White Masks* depicts the peculiarities of this situation by staging debates with Hegelian and post-Hegelian narratives of desire and recognition. Repeatedly the text is forced to conclude, despite the recalcitrant universalism of its author, that the object of its discourse, the colonial situation, 'is not a classic one'; that this situation imposes upon its subjects 'an existential deviation'; and that a signal index of this disabling deviation is that 'the black person has no ontological resistance to the white gaze' ([1952] 1967, pp. 225, 16, 110, translation revised): the colonised subject is politically disempowered from playing the game of human agency. 'Concerning Violence' says the same thing when it avers that it is in the formal logic of Aristotle's *Categories*, not in the dialectical logic of Hegel's *Phenomenology*, that we will find the open secret of the colonial relation.[3]

Notes

This chapter initially appeared as a section of chapter two ('Immediate Knowledge', pp. 55–72 and 250–52) under the subsection title 'Aristotle as Witness', in *Fanon's Dialectic of Experience* by Ato Sekyi-Otu, Cambridge, Mass.: Harvard University Press, Copyright © 1996 by the President and Fellows of Harvard College.

1 Charles Lam Markmann translates this chapter's title as 'The Fact of Blackness' (Fanon [1952] 1967).

2 In 1967, Josie Fanon (Fanon's widow, then living in Algeria) would order the removal of Sartre's Preface from subsequent editions of *Les damnés de la terre* published by Éditions Maspero, because of Sartre's support of Israel in the Arab-Israeli conflict. The Preface reappears in a 1991 edition *of Les damnés de la terre* published by Gallimard.

3 This critique of the principle of dialectical contradiction which Fanon's texts stage as a situational and strategic necessity has found a systematic epistemological statement in Lucio Colletti (1975, pp. 3–29). For a differentiation of the logic of antagonism from the concepts of contradiction and opposition, see Ernesto Laclau and Chantal Mouffe (1985, pp. 93–148).

References

Aristotle (1941). 'Categories'. In *The Basic Works of Aristotle*, edited and with an Introduction by Richard McKeon. New York: Random House.

Colletti, Lucio (1975). 'Marxism and the dialectic'. *New Left Review* 93: 3–29.

Fanon, Frantz (1952). *Peau noire, masques blancs*. Paris: Editions du Seuil.

Fanon, Frantz (1961). *Les damnés de la terre*. Paris: Découverte Poche.

Fanon, Frantz (1967). *Black Skin, White Masks* (1952). Translated by Charles Lam Markmann. New York: Grove Press.

Fanon, Frantz (1991). *The Wretched of the Earth* (1961). Translated by Constance Farrington. New York: Grove Press.

Gendzier, Irene L. (1973). *Frantz Fanon: A Critical Study*. New York: Pantheon.

Hegel, Georg Wilhelm Friedrich (1969). *The Science of Logic* (1812–1816). Translated by A.V. Miller. London: Oxford University Press.

Hegel, Georg Wilhelm Friedrich (1971). 'Love' (1797 or 1798). In Georg Wilhelm Friedrich Hegel, *On Christianity: Early Theological Writings*. Translated by Thomas Malcolm Knox. Philadelphia: University of Pennsylvania Press.

Hegel, Georg Wilhelm Friedrich (1977). *Hegel's Phenomenology of Spirit* (1807). Translated by A.V. Miller. Oxford: Clarendon Press.

Heidegger, Martin (1962). *Being and Time* (1927). Translated by John Macquarrie and Edward Robinson. New York: Harper and Row.

Laclau, Ernesto and Mouffe, Chantal (1985). *Hegemony and Socialist Strategy: Towards a Radical Democratic Politics*. Translated by Winston Moore and Paul Cammack. London: Verso.

Marx, Karl (1975a). 'Contribution to the critique of Hegel's philosophy of law' (1843). In Karl Marx and Friedrich Engels, *Collected Works*, vol. 3. Translated by Jack Cohen, Richard Dixon, Clemens Dutt et al. New York: International Publishers.

Marx, Karl (1975b). 'Economic and philosophic manuscripts of 1844' (1844). In Karl Marx and Friedrich Engels, *Collected Works*, vol. 3. Translated by Jack Cohen, Richard Dixon, Clemens Dutt et al. New York: International Publishers.

McBride, William Leon (1969). 'Sartre and the phenomenology of social violence'. In James M. Edie (ed.), *New Essays in Phenomenology*. Chicago: Quadrangle.

Memmi, Albert (1967). *The Colonizer and the Colonized* (1957). Translated by Howard Greenfeld. Boston: Beacon Press.

Ricoeur, Paul (1970). *History and Truth* (1955). Translated by Charles A. Kelbley. Evanston, Ill.: Northwestern University Press.

Sartre, Jean-Paul (1951). *Black Orpheus* (1948). Translated by Samuel W. Allen. Paris: Présence Africaine.

Sartre, Jean-Paul (1963). *Search for a Method* (1957). Translated by Hazel E. Barnes. New York: Vintage.

Sartre, Jean-Paul (1969). *Being and Nothingness* (1943). Translated by Hazel E. Barnes. New York: Washington Square Press.

Sartre, Jean-Paul (1978). *Critique of Dialectical Reason* (1960). Translated by Alan Sheridan-Smith, edited by Jonathan Rée. London: NLB.

Sartre, Jean-Paul (1991). 'Preface' (1961). In Frantz Fanon, *The Wretched of the Earth*. Translated by Constance Farrington. Harmondsworth: Penguin.

Schroyer, Trent (1973). *The Critique of Domination*. New York: George Braziller.

Senghor, Léopold Sédar (1948). *Anthologie de la nouvelle poésie nègre et malgache de langue française*. Paris: Presses universitaires de France.

Stern, Joseph Peter (1978). *Nietzsche*. Glasgow: Fontana/Collins.

Zahar, Renate (1970). *L'oeuvre de Frantz Fanon*. Translated from the German by Roger Dangeville. Paris: Éditions Maspero.

2 | Through Alexandre Kojève's Lens: Violence and the Dialectic of Lordship and Bondage in Frantz Fanon's *Black Skin, White Masks*

Philippe Van Haute

I n her famous text *On Violence*, Hannah Arendt severely criticises Frantz Fanon's 'glorification' of violence (Arendt 1970, pp. 14, 20, 65 *et passim*). Arendt rejects the idea that humans can only create themselves through violent action (1970, p. 12). Violence can be necessary or inevitable, but in no way is it essential to the liberation of the oppressed. However, this seems exactly what Fanon is suggesting. Even if violence cannot, for him, be an end in itself, it remains what Alice Cherki in her 2002 Preface to *Les damnés de la terre* calls 'an obligatory passage' (Cherki 2002, p. 11). This passage is not only necessary for empirical reasons. These empirical reasons can be quite real: how to respond to the violence of colonialism except by using counter-violence to break its rule? But Fanon goes further than this. In *Black Skin, White Masks* he writes: 'Thus human reality in-itself-for-itself can be achieved only through conflict and through the risk that conflict implies' (Fanon [1952] 2008, p. 170). And he continues in *The Wretched of the Earth* (and this is only one example): 'The colonized subject discovers reality and transforms it through his praxis, his deployment of violence and his agenda for liberation' (Fanon [1961] 2004, p. 44). Revolutionary praxis is here virtually identified with the use of violence for what seem to be essential reasons, thus making Arendt's critique at least plausible.

In this chapter, I wish to unearth the underlying *logic* that determines the place of violence in Fanon's thinking, particularly in *Black Skin, White Masks* (Fanon [1952] 2008) and in *The Wretched of the Earth* (Fanon [1961] 2004), by showing how this logic has a fundamentally Hegelian – or more specifically Kojèvian – character. More specifically, I will argue that the central place of violence in Fanon's thinking is intrinsically linked to his reading of Alexandre Kojève who, in turn, provides a very specific reading of Georg Wilhelm Friedrich Hegel.

In *Black Skin, White Masks*, Fanon discusses only two authors in a more or less systematic way: Octave Mannoni and Hegel (or, more specifically, the latter's dialectic of lordship and bondage).[1] In a section entitled 'The Negro and Hegel', Fanon explicitly aims to show that the dialectic of lordship and bondage as Hegel developed it in his *Phenomenology of Spirit* (Hegel [1807] 1977) does not apply to the social relations that exist under colonial rule (Fanon [1952] 2008, pp. 167–73). Fanon's chapter on Hegel does not contain a rigorous *Auseinandersetzung* (confrontation) with Hegel's conceptualisation. Rather, it contains scattered notes that would still need to be structured and explained for the (in large part implicit) argumentation to become clearer.

But while trying to make sense of Fanon's critical reading of the dialectic of lordship and bondage, anybody who is even vaguely familiar with Hegel's text would soon realise that Fanon's interpretation does not apply to the corresponding chapter in *The Phenomenology of Spirit*. This does not mean that it does not make sense; it means that Fanon reads Hegel in a very peculiar 'French' way. Or more concretely, Fanon reads Hegel *through Kojève's lens*. Kojève's reading of Hegel indeed dominated the French philosophical scene from the nineteen-thirties until (at least) the nineteen-seventies. Whenever a French philosopher said 'Hegel,' she meant, knowingly or not, 'Kojève'. Fanon is no exception in this regard.

Some general remarks on *The Phenomenology of Spirit*

Hegel's *Phenomenology* describes how consciousness, starting from its most humble form – 'sense-certainty', that is, receptivity to what is as it is, without interpretation of any kind (Hegel [1807] 1977, p. 58 – §66) – progressively gets access to absolute knowledge. This progressive evolution passes through a series of 'shapes of consciousness' – such as the lord–bondsman dialectic. Every one of these shapes contains, in principle, a theory of knowledge that determines what true knowledge consists of. At the same time, this theory elucidates the way in which consciousness understands itself at a particular level of its development. However, time and again it becomes clear that the object as it is defined in the theory does not correspond to the object as it is experienced or known. A short illustration can make clear what I mean. Consciousness first defines knowledge (and itself) as pure sense-certainty. Hegel analyses sense-certainty as an immediate grasp of what is as it is. His analysis then mainly turns around the distinction between this level of immediacy and the language – primarily indexicals such as 'here', 'now' and 'this' – in which we articulate what we know. In other words, Hegel starts from the distinction between the object ('this'), the demonstrative pronoun that refers to what is simply present to consciousness, and what we mean when we use such demonstrative pronouns. It immediately becomes clear that we cannot say what we mean, since language situates what we mean at the level of generality, whereas what we mean is at this stage defined as a particular that is immediately given in sensation (*sense*-certainty). There is a distinction between what is given in experience and these demonstrative pronouns that can be falsified by observation: what is 'here' at one moment can be 'there' at another, depending on the position of the subject. In this way it becomes progressively clearer that knowledge depends on the subject, and cannot be reduced to an immediate grasp of what is given as such. The examination of the subject-pole further makes clear that knowledge cannot depend on a particular subject. Knowledge depends on 'the I as universal': '[sense]-certainty experiences ... that its essence is neither in the object, nor in the I, and immediacy is neither the immediacy of one or the other; for in both what we mean is rather inessential, *and the object and the I are universal*' (Hegel [1807] 1977, p. 62 – §103; emphasis added).

Hegel concludes from his complex analysis that knowledge is not and cannot be immediate (it is not about particulars known by a particular subject), but is essentially mediate (about general properties that are known by a universal subject): 'I take it (the object) up as it is in truth, and instead of knowing an immediacy, *I perceive it*' (Hegel [1807] 1977, p. 66 – §110, emphasis added).

The most important aspect of his analysis for my purpose here is that every change in the object-pole – we do not know what is immediately given; we only know general properties – is accompanied by a redefinition of consciousness. The latter is not just receptive but is active itself. Hence, sense-certainty is redefined as perception. Every shape of consciousness implies a redefinition of the subject-pole in its intrinsic relation to the object-pole (Hegel [1807] 1977, p. 54 – §85). Epistemology and ontology go hand in hand in this process (Rockmore 1997). Consciousness's progressive understanding of what true knowledge entails inevitably implies a growing insight into the fundamental structures of being and of itself. Both aspects are intrinsically interwoven. At the end of the process, consciousness understands not just the nature of true knowledge, but also the essence of (the totality of) being. The *Phenomenology* then describes how this process is accomplished through consciousness's own experience (Hegel [1807] 1977, p. 21 – §36): phenomenology is the *Wissenschaft der Erfahrung des Bewusstseins* (science of the experience of consciousness). It is a science because this process responds to an inevitable logic that can be thematised as such. The *Phenomenology* has to be understood as a *Bildungsroman*: it describes how consciousness, *on the basis of its own experience*, progressively gets access to true (absolute) knowledge ([1807] 1977, p. 50 – §78). As a result, the truth and significance of the successive shapes of consciousness only become clear at the end of their development. This also implies that no particular shape of consciousness – such as the dialectic of lord and bondsman – can be used to understand the process as a whole. For this reason alone, Kojève's (Heideggerian and Marxist) interpretation (Kojève [1947] 1980), which states that the dialectic of lord and bondsman – in Kojève's terms, the *maître* (master) and the *esclave* (slave) – unveils the fundamental dynamics of history in the *Phenomenology*, is highly problematic.

It follows that we have to distinguish three types of consciousness when reading the *Phenomenology*. There is, firstly, the 'natural' consciousness that we know already. It is the *'naïf'* consciousness that time and again thinks it knows the object as it is, and that time and again has to realise that this is not case. The second type of consciousness is 'philosophical' consciousness; it refers to the philosopher – Hegel in the first place – who is already at the level of absolute knowledge and from whose standpoint the *Phenomenology* is written. Last but not least, there is the 'phenomenological' consciousness that accompanies the adventure of natural consciousness. This is the consciousness that defines the reader of the *Phenomenology* (Cobben 1996, p. 35).

Lordship and bondage in *The Phenomenology of Spirit*

Part B of *The Phenomenology of Spirit* on 'Self-Consciousness' starts with the observation that consciousness has already learned from its previous experiences that the object of cognition is dependent on its own actions (Hegel [1807] 1977, pp. 137–40 – §§ 164–66). In very general terms, we could say that consciousness has now reached an epistemological standpoint characterised by Kant's transcendental philosophy: whatever truth of reality the subject is capable of calling to mind is due not to its passive perception of reality (as in sense-certainty), but to an act of consciousness that has already constituted the alleged 'object' (Honneth 2012, p. 5). Hence, in the object 'I' know myself. This is why Hegel writes: 'But now there has arisen what did not emerge in these previous relationships (sense-certainty...), viz. a certainty which is identical to its truth; *for the certainty is to itself its own object, and consciousness is to itself the truth'* (Hegel [1807] 1977, p. 102 – §166, emphasis added).

Hegel further specifies this self-consciousness: in a first moment, it understands itself as a pure tautology in which there is no place for anything but itself: 'As self-consciousness, it is movement; but since what it distinguishes from itself is only itself as itself, the difference, as an otherness, is *immediately superseded* for it; *the difference is not, and it [self-consciousness] is only the motionless tautology of: "I am I"*; but since for it the difference *does not have the form of being,* it is *not* self-consciousness' (Hegel [1807] 1977, p. 105 – §167, emphasis added).

In this first tautological moment, the external object (difference as 'otherness', difference as a 'form of being') seems to be lost. Self-consciousness does not understand itself, in this first moment of its appearance to itself, as a unity with consciousness (that is, as essentially a relation to an object that is not just itself). The object only appears to self-consciousness as an otherness that has no real existence of its own ('does not have the form of being').

One should think here of the way in which the experiencing (natural) consciousness relates to its own development. Natural consciousness is not aware of its own history. Hence, it does not understand its experience as a continuous and necessary teleological process. It does not grasp or understand itself as the outcome of the previous shapes of consciousness. This is precisely what the further development of self-consciousness is about. Self-consciousness has to 'remember' its history or, what essentially comes down to the same thing, it has to recover its relation to the object – 'difference that has the form of being' – but without giving up the outcome or the result of the previous development. This object will no longer be outside of (self-)consciousness, as was still the case in sense-certainty, for example. It will be a difference that at the same time is not. It will be an object that no longer falls outside of self-consciousness. We will see that it is precisely in and through this development that self-consciousness can attain its active role as an originator of reality outside itself.

All of this remains very abstract and needs further explication. In order to embark on such explication, let us return to Hegel's text. In a first move, Hegel establishes the presuppositions – conditions for this recovery of consciousness – of the object. How must we conceive of self-consciousness, for this recovery of the object – the overcoming of the mere tautology of the I = I – to be possible? In a second move, he shows how natural consciousness can have access to these presuppositions through its own experiences.

Hegel mentions two crucial conditions that have to be fulfilled if self-consciousness is ever to recover the object that it seems to have lost. Self-consciousness needs to be corporeal; and it only exists as a relation to others. In other words, self-consciousness is *qua* self-consciousness both corporeal and social. Hegel has already introduced 'life' as a theme at the end of the previous chapter on consciousness (Hegel [1807] 1977, p. 100 – §162). In the chapter on self-consciousness, he builds on his previous reflections and stresses the fact that self-consciousness can only exist as itself participating in the movement of life. It is in this context that he characterises self-consciousness as *desire*.

Desire forces self-consciousness out into the world. There is no relation to the outside world except through the senses or, what comes down to the same thing, through the body. The body, Hegel continues, is essentially desire, and more particularly desire of a living object. The relation to this object is in the first instance essentially negative:[2]

> This antithesis of its appearance and its truth has, however, for its essence only the truth, viz. the unity of self-consciousness with itself; this unity must become essential to self-consciousness; i.e. *self-consciousness is Desire in general. Consciousness, as self-consciousness, henceforth has a double object: one is the immediate object, that of sense-certainty and perception, which however for self-consciousness has the character of the negative; and the second, viz. itself, which is the true essence,* and is present in the first instance only as opposed to the first object. In this sphere, self-consciousness exhibits itself as the movement in which this antithesis is removed, and the identity of itself with itself becomes explicit for it. (Hegel [1807] 1977, p. 109 – §174, emphasis added)

This quotation from the *Phenomenology* clearly indicates that self-consciousness has a double object: itself and the outside objects (the realm of 'life' and of bodily existence) to which it relates in an exclusively negative way (they are what self-consciousness is *not*). As a result, at this stage of its development, self-consciousness does not understand itself as essentially a living (corporeal) being. The latter is indeed what needs to be sublated (a process that could also be understood in terms of physical annihilation) for the I to realise its identity with itself. As long as self-consciousness understands itself exclusively as the tautology of the I = I (as already mentioned), the body can only be what self-consciousness is *not*. At this stage, self-consciousness represents a Cartesian position, as it were: it is not its body, but rather a pure relation to itself that does not need anything else to exist.

From these considerations, one thing already becomes clear: desire (*Begierde*) in the Hegelian sense can at no point of the development be equated with animal desire as Kojève – and apparently Fanon – would have it. Desire is, on the contrary, always already a 'spiritual' principle: it is essentially self-consciousness establishing the tautology of the 'I am I' through negating the object (Cruysberghs 1983; Jenkins 2009).

But before developing this problematic any further – and explaining its importance for the present debate – let us remain with Hegel for a moment. Whatever self-consciousness as desire tries to do, the object that is sublated constantly returns. The negation never completely succeeds. When I eat an animal to satisfy my desire, the hunger inevitably returns, and with it the relation to an object that needs to be negated.

At this point, a crucial development occurs: if the object cannot be destroyed – or rather, if the object cannot be permanently metabolised as part of the self (that is when it always resurfaces) – on the one hand, and if self-consciousness has to recognise itself in it on the other (since it does not know anything outside itself at this stage), the object has to be another self-consciousness for self-consciousness to be possible.[3] Hence self-consciousness is not only corporeal, it is also essentially social and relational. It only exists in and through the recognition of another self-consciousness (Hegel [1807] 1977, p. 111 – §178).

However, it is not enough that the philosophical and phenomenological consciousness knows that self-consciousness is an essentially bodily and social reality. Natural (self-)consciousness has to find this out for itself in and through its own experience. The question Hegel has to answer then is: how is this possible? How does self-consciousness get access to the truth of what *we* – the philosopher and the consciousness that accompanies the experience of natural consciousness – know already? It is at this point that Hegel introduces the life-and-death struggle and the dialectic of lord and bondsman. We are approaching our goal.

Let us take a close look at Hegel's text here, because this is crucial to a proper understanding of its dynamic:

> Self-consciousness is, to begin with, simple being-for-self, self equal through the exclusion from itself of everything else. For it, its essence and absolute object is 'I'; and in this immediacy, or in this [mere] being, of its being-for-self, it is an individual. *What is 'other' for it is an unessential, negatively characterized object. But the 'other' is also a self-consciousness* ... Appearing thus immediately on the scene, *they are for one another like ordinary objects, they have not as yet exposed themselves to each other in the form of pure being-for-self, or as self-consciousnesses* ... ([1807] 1977, p. 113 – §186, emphasis added)

This is how, in the first instance, both self-consciousnesses – both defined as desire (as explained above) – relate to one another: each one of them appears to the other as an ordinary object which, like all the other objects, has to be annihilated. A life-and-death struggle is the inevitable result of this. The struggle is, in other words, the result of the fact that both self-consciousnesses consider each other as mere (living) objects. The struggle does not find its origin in a supposed '*desire for* recognition'.[4] The two self-consciousnesses do not start their fight because they want to be recognised by each other. Hegel writes:

> This presentation is a twofold action: action on the part of the other, and action on its own part. In so far as it is the action of the other, each seeks the death of the other. But in doing so, the second kind of action, action on its own part, is also involved; for the former involves the staking of its own life. *Thus, the relation of the two self-conscious individuals is such that they prove themselves and each other through a life-and-death struggle.* ([1807] 1977, p. 113–114 – §187, emphasis added)

This life-and-death struggle is necessary because it is only in and through this fight that both self-consciousnessess can show to each other and to themselves that this is exactly what they are: 'pure being for itself' (pure negativity) in which 'there is nothing present ... which could not be regarded as a vanishing moment' ([1807] 1977, p. 114 – §187). But, once again, even if it is crucial to us (that is, to the generic philosopher) that it is two equal self-consciousnesses that relate to each other, these self-consciousnesses do not recognise each other as (potentially) self-consciousness prior to the fight. It is only in and through the fight that they can appear to each other as pure 'for itself'. Hegel states:

> *They must engage in this struggle, for they must raise their certainty of being for themselves to truth, both in the case of the other and in their own case.* And it is only through staking one's life that ... it [is] proved that for self-consciousness ... its essential being is not (just) the immediate form in which it appears, not its submergence in the expanse of life, but rather that there is nothing present in it which could not be regarded as a vanishing moment, that it is only pure being-for-self. ([1807] 1977, p. 114 – §187, emphasis added)

However, self-consciousness comes to realise that life is as essential to it as the absolute negation: *'In this experience, self-consciousness learns that life is as essential to it as pure self-consciousness'* ([1807] 1977, p. 115 – §189, emphasis added). Precisely for this reason, one of the two self-consciousnesses surrenders. It prefers life over the negating power of self-consciousness. It becomes a 'bondsman' – and not a 'slave' (*'Sklave'*) as we used to say – working for the 'lord'. In this way, self-consciousness becomes aware *on the basis of its own experience,* and be it in a still very formal way, that it is essentially 'corporeal' and that it can only exist in a society under the rule of law (lordship).

Hegel is not describing a real or historical situation, let alone slavery as it existed in his day. The translation of *'Herr'* as *'maître'* (master) and *'Knecht'* as *'esclave'* (slave), as we find it in Kojève, obviously facilitates such an interpretation. There is no immediate historical equivalent to the dialectic of lordship and bondage. The passages I am discussing here are not about a concrete historical relation. They do not analyse the dynamics or the underlying driving forces – one can think here of the desire for recognition or the contradictions that inhabit the forces and relations of production – that would determine the development of such a relation and the course of history. Hegel is not thinking here of the history of socio-political oppression and liberation as such; his perspective is epistemological and ontological, not socio-political. For him, the lord and the bondsman represent two essential aspects of self-consciousness that still need to be unified. This is fundamentally also why at this level of the *Phenomenology* – or in this shape of consciousness – not all conditions have yet been fulfilled for a concrete historical existence.[5]

Leaving out some essential elements, we can summarise the situation with which we are confronted at this point of Hegel's analysis as follows: on the one hand, there is the lord who was prepared to continue the fight, and in doing so proved that he is nothing but absolute negation;[6] on the other hand, there is the bondsman who preferred life over death, and who is now placed between the lord and the world of objects. The independence and irreducibility of the object does not pose a problem for the lord. The bondsman deals with it by working for him ([1807]

1977, p. 116 – §190). The lord does not really recognise this bondsman as a self-consciousness ([1807] 1977, p. 116 – §192). How could he, since the bondsman, unlike the lord, preferred life and in doing so abdicated as a 'pure for itself'?

The bondsman sees in the lord the 'pure for itself' that he was not up to ([1807] 1977, p. 117 – §194). At the same time, the bondsman has this 'for itself' ('*für sich*') also 'in itself' ('*an sich*'). In the fear of death the bondsman is afraid not for this or that particular object or aspect of it, but for his life as such that *cannot* be reduced to any specific aspect that makes life worthwhile to him ([1807] 1977, p. 117 – §194). Hence the bondsman experiences the 'fluidity of the differences or their general dissolution' ([1807] 1977, p. 108 – §171) that he sees or observes in the lord in his own bodily existence.

This 'in itself' and 'for itself' have to be united, and this is precisely where the role of 'work' comes in. Indeed, the bondsman works for the lord. Hegel writes in this regard:

> Work, on the other hand, is desire held in check, fleetingness staved off; in other words, *work forms and shapes the thing. The negative relation to the object becomes its form* and something permanent, because it is precisely for the worker that the object has independence ... *It is in this way, therefore, that consciousness, qua worker [das arbeitende Bewusstsein], comes to see in the independent being [of the object] its own independence.* ([1807] 1977, p. 118 – §195, emphasis added)

I will leave the frivolous translation of '*das arbeitende Bewusstsein*' ('working consciousness') as 'worker' in this passage for what it is – frivolous – and focus instead on the shape of self-consciousness that Hegel sees developing in the bondsman. The bondsman carries the negativity of self-consciousness in itself (*an sich*, which in this context means 'potentially'); he can realise or actualise this negativity in the world of objects in and through his work (for the lord). As a result, this world receives *the form* of self-consciousness. The negativity of self-consciousness is, as it were, inscribed in the world through the work of the bondsman, so that from now on self-consciousness knows itself in the object. Self-consciousness and consciousness (the relation to the object) are united now. The object is no longer *outside* of self-consciousness: 'We are in the presence of self-consciousness in a new shape, *a consciousness which, as the infinitude of consciousness or as its own pure movement, is aware of itself as essential being, a being which thinks or is a free self-consciousness'* ([1807] 1977, p. 120 – §197, emphasis added).

In and through 'work', self-consciousness attains its active role as an originator of reality outside of itself: in and through work, the world of objects receives the form of negativity that characterises self-consciousness. From now on, self-consciousness – at least in principle – knows itself in knowing the object. This is what Hegel calls *freedom*. And this freedom has to be understood primarily in an ontological, not in a socio-political way.

From all of this it becomes clear that to simply apply Hegel's text on lordship and bondage to the colonial relation between a master and a slave goes against Hegel's explicit intentions with regard to the shapes of consciousness under consideration. The question as to whether the relation between lordship and bondage, as Hegel described it, fits the colonial situation turns this relation into something that it is not and, for the reasons I have explained above, cannot be – namely an analysis of a concrete historical situation.

The relation is differently stated, however, in the famous interpretation that Kojève gave of this text, which had a defining impact on the French philosophical scene until at least the nineteen-sixties. Kojève turned the dialectics between what he calls a 'master' (*'maître'*) and a 'slave' (*'esclave'*) into the royal road to the understanding of *The Phenomenology of Spirit* as a whole. Hegel's *Phenomenology*, according to Kojève, describes the history of humankind as a history of ongoing conflict between masters and slaves, driven by a fundamental desire for recognition that ends with the overcoming of the fundamental opposition at stake. Kojève writes:

> ... that history must be the history of the interaction between Mastery and Slavery: *the historical 'dialectic' is the 'dialectic' of Mastery and Slavery*. But if the opposition of 'thesis' and 'antithesis' is meaningful only in the context of their reconciliation by 'synthesis', if history (in the full sense of the word) necessarily has a final term, if man who becomes must culminate in man who has become, if Desire must end in satisfaction, if the science of man must possess the quality of a definitively and universally valid truth – *the interaction of Master and Slave must finally end in the 'dialectical overcoming' of both of them*. (Kojève [1947] 1980, p. 9, emphasis added)

Kojève's reference to 'Mastery and Slavery' provides a prima facie justification for confronting Hegel's analysis of lordship and bondage with actually existing slavery in the colonial context. Hegel does not speak of slavery (*Sklaverei*) in the contexts I am discussing here. On the contrary, when he speaks of slavery as a specific social institution he does write '*Sklaverei*' (Hegel [1821] 1955, p. 65 – §57). The translation of 'bondsman' as 'slave' seems to open the door to establishing a link with crucial aspects of the colonial reality.

Kojève and Fanon on the master–slave dialectic

It is indeed Kojève who, probably both directly and indirectly (via Jean-Paul Sartre and Simone de Beauvoir), inspired Fanon's reading of Hegel in the chapter on 'The Negro and Hegel' at the end of *Black Skin, White Masks* (Fanon [1952] 2008, pp. 168–73). Kojève starts from a decisive distinction between 'animal' desire and human desire for recognition – that is, desire for the desire of the other (Kojève [1947] 1980, pp. 6–7). Desire, Kojève writes, is anthropogenic when it takes another desire as its object. Self-consciousness has to prove that 'life' is not its highest value. It has to transcend animal desire. This is only possible through a struggle without any vital aim, a 'fight to the death for pure prestige' (Kojève [1947] 1980, p. 7). Only if I 'prove' that life is not my highest value, can I be fully recognised as self-consciousness. Self-consciousness in the full sense of the word can only be realised by putting one's life on the line in the pursuit of recognition by the other.

At this point, Fanon still seems to be in complete agreement with Kojève's anthropological reading of Hegel's *Phenomenology*. The first lines of the chapter on 'The Negro and Hegel' indeed read as follows:

> *Man is human only to the extent to which he tries to impose his existence on another man in order to be recognized by him* ... As soon as I desire I am asking to be considered ... I demand that notice be taken of my negating activity insofar as *I pursue something other than life; insofar as I do battle for the creation of a human world – that is, of a world of reciprocal recognitions*. (Fanon [1952] 2008, pp. 168, 170, emphasis added)

The difference between this passage and Hegel's text is clearly visible. For Kojève – and Fanon seems to follow him here – desire for recognition is the essential characteristic of the human being, and transcending animal desire our most urgent task as humans. From a strictly Hegelian perspective this is highly problematic. In very general terms, Hegel does not develop an anthropology in *The Phenomenology of Spirit*. But apart from that, 'desire' for Hegel is not animal desire. It is always already self-consciousness. In his text, overcoming animal desire is a non-issue. Furthermore, Kojève interprets the life-and-death struggle as the starting point of a social dialectics across a history determined by a continuous fight for recognition between 'masters' and 'slaves'. Fanon seems to take this interpretation – and this translation – for granted. Only from this (anthropological and Marxist) perspective does it make sense to speak of a 'battle for the creation ... of a world of reciprocal recognitions' (Fanon [1952] 2008, p. 170) in reference to Hegel's dialectic of lordship and bondage, or to compare the Hegelian master and slave with the colonial relation, as Fanon does ([1952] 2008, p. 172).

It is in this context that Fanon claims that Hegel's depiction of the master–slave relation does not fit the relation between the master-coloniser and the slave-colonised. The following short passage taken from a footnote in Fanon's chapter summarises his central intuition in this regard: 'For Hegel there is reciprocity; here the master laughs at the consciousness of the slave. What he wants from the slave is not recognition, but work' ([1952] 2008, p. 172 n. 8).

At first sight, Kojève seems to be stating something similar. He claims that '[the slave] must "recognize" the other without being "recognized"' (Kojève [1947] 1980, pp. 19, 224). He further states that the master '(sees) in the beginning ... in the other only the aspect of an animal' ([1947] 1980, p. 13). For the master, the slave is nothing but 'a living corpse' ([1947] 1980, p. 16). So what can Fanon be thinking of when he claims that *in contradistinction* to Hegel and Kojève, there is no reciprocity in the colonial master–slave relation?

Fanon's claim only makes sense on the basis of some implicit presuppositions that are not to be found literally stated in his text, but that we have to reconstruct. Hence, an interpretation of these passages can only be tentative. What implicit presuppositions am I talking about? For Kojève, the structure of domination is a *result* of the initial struggle. For Hegel this struggle does not presuppose that both self-consciousnesses involved recognise each other one way or the other as 'equals' prior to the fight. On the contrary, their struggle starts because they do not yet see each other as self-consciousnesses. But for Kojève things are more ambiguous. On the one hand, he states that at the beginning of the fight, both protagonists only see in the other 'the aspect of the animal' ([1947] 1980, p. 13). But on the other hand, he claims that this struggle originates in a desire for recognition. Such a struggle for recognition can only start if both partners recognise each other in some way as potentially human (Kleinberg 2003, p. 121). We can only be interested in being recognised by another living being when this being is already considered to belong to the 'same genus' as we do. Whatever the historical vicissitudes of the unequal relation that results from the struggle, this 'proto-recognition'

(Kleinberg 2003, p. 121) guarantees that both parties essentially belong to the *same* history. There is, as it were, a primordial inclusion without which the master–slave dialectic cannot begin, and without which both parties cannot belong to a history that inevitably and essentially aims at the realisation of a universal and reciprocal recognition, as Kojève – and Fanon – think it does.

In Fanon's implicit logic, however, the structure of domination seems to *precede* the struggle for recognition. But if the structure of domination precedes the fight, then the primordial inclusion referred to above does not seem to be guaranteed. It is indeed true that in the fight between the slave and the master, both have experienced the fear of death;[7] this experience can in a certain sense be considered to be the objective ('in itself') ground for what I called a primordial inclusion that precedes the fight. It ensures from the outset that *both* the master and the slave participate in the absolute negativity that characterises self-consciousness. They have both experienced the same fear, although the master has decided not to give in to it, whereas the slave was too attached to his life to do the same. However, if we take it that the life-and-death struggle follows the structure of domination, this inclusion is not given from the outset. I take it that this is what Fanon means when he claims that 'the master just laughs at the consciousness of the slave'. For the colonial master, the slave does not participate in a common history. The latter belongs to a 'new genus'. Fanon writes: 'And already I am being dissected under white eyes, the only real eyes. I am fixed. Having adjusted their microtomes, they objectively cut away slices of my reality. I am laid bare. I feel, I see in those white faces that it is not a new man who has come in, but a new kind of man, *a new genus*. Why, it's a Negro' ([1952] 2008, p. 87, emphasis added).

According to Fanon, the colonial master at no point wants recognition from the slave, with whom he thinks furthermore to have nothing in common. The colonial master only wants the slave to work; the slave is a mere replaceable instrument with whom the master has none other than an external (instrumental) link.[8] The crucial question now becomes why 'work' cannot play a dialectical and liberating role here in the same way as it does in the Kojèvian or Hegelian dialectic.[9]

Here again, Fanon gives no further explanation of what he means. He gives no particular weight to work in the dialectical process; for him it does not play a formative role. We can try to reconstruct his argument as follows. For Hegel and Kojève, work can only play a liberating role on condition that the slave has also experienced the fear of death. It is precisely in and through this fear, Kojève writes, that the slave realises that a given and stable condition, albeit the master's, cannot exhaust the possibilities of human existence. As a result, the slave is ready for change. He is ready to constantly transcend and transform himself. He is historical becoming in his very essence (Kojève [1947] 1980, p. 22). This change and self-transformation takes place in and through the work he is forced to do for the master. Its historical and formative significance remains unintelligible apart from its mediation of the fear of death ([1947] 1980, p. 23). For Kojève (and Hegel) the ontological and anthropological meaning of work and the experience of the death in the life-and-death struggle are intrinsically linked. Kojève concludes:

> The Slave, in transforming the given World by his work, transcends the given and what is given by that given in himself; hence, he goes beyond himself, and also goes beyond the Master who is tied to the given which, not working, he leaves intact. *If the fear of death, incarnated for the Slave in the person of the warlike Master, is the sine qua non of historical progress, it is solely the Slave's work that realizes and perfects it.* ([1947] 1980, p. 23, emphasis added)

For Fanon, however, the fight and the experience of absolute negativity that characterises self-consciousness have not yet taken place. In terms of the Hegelian-Kojèvian logic, this means that work can only have an instrumental meaning without any liberating potential.

The place of violence in *Black Skin, White Masks*

From what I have explained thus far, it becomes clear that – from Fanon's Kojèvian perspective – violence is bound to become a crucial anthropological category and the motor force of the revolutionary dialectic. On the one hand, Fanon implies that domination precedes the fight; on the other hand – and simultaneously – he sticks to the Kojèvian idea that the life-and-death struggle is essentially anthropogenic. From this perspective, it comes as no surprise – rather, it follows almost logically – that the slave, in order to become a human being in the full sense of the word for the master and for himself, has to risk his life in a life-and-death struggle. Once one removes the dialectical meaning from work, in a Kojèvian context only violence remains as the motor of a history aiming at a world in which the opposition between masters and slaves is overcome, and universal reciprocal recognition is achieved. The following passages from *Black Skin, White Masks* illustrate this idea:

> The former slave needs a challenge to his humanity, he wants a conflict, a riot. (Fanon [1952] 2008, p. 172)
> The Negro knows nothing of the cost of freedom, for he has not fought for it. Occasionally he has fought for liberty and justice, but always white liberty and white justice, that is, the values secreted by the masters. ([1952] 2008, p. 172)

This idea is also expressed in *The Wretched of the Earth*: 'The colonized subject discovers reality and transforms it through his praxis, his deployment of violence and his agenda for liberation' (Fanon [1961] 2004, p.44).

We can now better understand the further developments of Fanon's argument. In Hegel, Fanon states, the slave cannot overcome his subordinate position without a fight; but in the (French) colonial situation, the slave has been set free by his master.[10] As a result, the black man has been deprived of the possibility of proving that he is an independent and autonomous self-consciousness to be recognised in his own right.

43

In this context, Fanon ([1961] 2004, p. 170) further refers to a rather obscure passage in Hegel which states that without having risked its life in the struggle for life-and-death, a self-consciousness can be recognised as a *person*, but not as a self-consciousness that has 'attained to the truth of this recognition as an independent self-consciousness' (Hegel [1807] 1977, p. 114 – §187). It is not exactly clear what Fanon means by referring to this passage, but I read it as follows: the recognition of the slave as a 'person' is merely formal and thus incomplete and false. For such a 'person', Fanon continues, the master can show at best a 'paternalistic curiosity' (Fanon [1952] 2008, p. 172). Clearly, just being 'set free' does not suffice. Freedom without a fight with the master is not worth much in the colonial situation.

But does the master not include the slave in his history by setting him free? Does the slave not participate from now on in a common history with the master? Not really: as a mere 'person' or 'recognizer', he can only be included on the condition and insofar as he remains subservient to and imitates the former (white) master:

> *The Negro wants to be like the master. Therefore he is less independent than the Hegelian slave.* ([1952] 2008, p. 172 n. 8, emphasis added)
> *The upheaval reached the black from without. The black was acted upon.* Values that had not been created by his actions, values that had not resulted from the systolic tide of his blood, danced in a colored whirl around him. ([1952] 2008, p. 171, emphasis added)

Once he has been set free by the coloniser, the black man *qua* person can only be included in as far as he becomes, or tries to become, identical with (as far as he tries to imitate) his former white master and gives up his difference. The Kojèvian slave, too, wants to be like the master in overcoming his fear of death and moving towards self-consciousness. But Fanon claims that in the colonial situation, we are talking about something essentially different: for the black person to be like the master, to take him as a model, means becoming white: 'This internalization of desirability of being white is a "form of recognition that Hegel had not envisaged"' (Gibson 2003, p. 37). This desire to be white blocks the dialectical movement that would lead to a true recognition as equals of both parties involved. Stated differently, in this way the interaction of 'master' and 'slave' can never end in the 'dialectical overcoming' of both of them (Kojève [1947] 1980, p. 9). For this to be possible, a violent upheaval is necessary – a conflict and a riot in and through which the slave affirms his humanity for its own sake and creates values resulting from the systolic tide of his own blood.

This is also the place where we can situate what Fanon – and we understand now: *against* Kojève – calls 'alienation' or 'cultural imposition': there is an ideological dimension that blocks the dialectical movement from developing towards the struggle for recognition. Colonised people (cannot but?) identify with the white man and take him as their model for what is good and essential. As a consequence, the black man 'has the same collective unconscious as the European ... After having been a slave to the white man, he enslaves himself' (Fanon [1952] 2008, p. 168). In other words, it is the 'fact of blackness' ([1952] 2008, pp. 82–108) and racism that leads to the elision of the dialectics of recognition from the colonial situation. The black person is not considered to be able to play an essential role in the course of history.

As I have argued in this chapter, Fanon's critique of what he calls the master–slave dialectic only makes sense from the perspective of Kojève's interpretation of it. In Hegel, the so-called dialectic of lordship and bondage deals with the progressive appearance of the ontological structure of self-consciousness and not with a concrete socio-historical situation or development driven by an anthropogenic desire for recognition.

Fanon's reading and critique of Hegel-Kojève had a huge impact on his thinking. It determined, more particularly, the crucial role of violence in his philosophy. In Hegel, the two (abstract) aspects of self-consciousness that are figured by the lord and the bondsman – and that result from the life-and-death fight – are integrated in the *work* of the bondsman. This integration implies a first formal realisation of (onto-logical) freedom and the introduction of a new shape of consciousness. In Kojève, the whole of human history is understood in terms of the master–slave dialectic. In this Marxist interpretation, the course of history is determined by the tensions that occur at the level of material (work-related) conditions of society. These tensions can (and quite often will) result in a violent overthrowing of existing social relations, but this violence has an instrumental meaning. Its exclusive role is to allow the historical process to free the potentialities inherent in the relations of production that determine the course of human history. But since the black man is excluded from this common history, work loses its liberating and revolutionary potential in the colonial situation. This explains the reversal with respect to Hegel and Kojève that takes place in Fanon's philosophy: for him, work has a purely instrumental mean-ing, and a violent revolution is the only possibility for the colonised to affirm him- or herself as a self-consciousness in his or her own right. Here violence attains an essential meaning (Arendt 1970). It is violence rather than work that constitutes the driving force of history. It is only by putting his life on the line that the slave can hope to overcome the colonial situation both for himself and for the (white) master.

This perspective allows us to understand the following passage from *Black Skin, White Masks*: 'the American Negro is cast in a different play. In the United States the Negro battles and is battled ... nothing is going to be given free ... On the field of battle ... a monument is slowly being built that promises to be majestic. And, at the top of this mon-ument, I can already see a white man and a black man hand in hand' (Fanon [1952] 2008, pp. 171–72).[11] Whereas the French colonial pow-ers – at least in Martinique – took away the possibility for the slave to really affirm himself as an independent self-consciousness in his own right, the American black man has to fight for his freedom. As a result – at least that is how I understand Fanon in this context – a dialectical development is possible that leads to a 'universal recognition' in which not only the opposition between 'masters' and 'slaves', but also the opposition between 'white' and 'black' can be overcome.

It becomes clear that Fanon's emphasis on the role and meaning of violence for the overcoming of the colonial relation is directly linked to the Kojèvian conceptualisation that underlies his work. Once one accepts this conceptualisation – and as long as one remains true to it – only a limited number of propositions can be made to understand the colonial situation and its overcoming. In other words, this conceptualisation inevitably predetermines the interpretation of the colonial situation and the possible ways for it to be overcome.

Conclusion

I have explained why 'work' loses its dialectical meaning in Fanon's (Kojèvian) thinking, and why this loss (inevitably?) leads to an (over) valuation of the role of the life-and-death struggle (and of violence) as the dialectical motor force of history and as an 'obligatory passage' ('*un passage obligé*', Cherki 2002, p. 11) towards universal recognition.[12] The way Fanon thematises this 'obligation' is absent from both Kojève and Hegel, for the reasons mentioned.

The reading I have proposed in this chapter would illuminate and situate the perspective on violence that we find in *The Wretched of the Earth*:

For the colonized, this violence represents the absolute praxis. The militant therefore is one who works ... To work means to work towards the death of the colonist. Claiming responsibility for the violence also allows those members of the group who have strayed or have been outlawed to come back, to retake their place and be reintegrated. Violence can thus be understood to be the perfect mediation. The colonized man liberates himself in and through violence. This praxis enlightens the militant because it shows him the means and the end. (Fanon [1961] 2004, p. 44)

The quasi-equation of praxis, work and violence can only be philosophically understood and examined from the perspective developed in this chapter. It is the direct result of a Kojèvian framework or conceptual logic that determines – wittingly or unwittingly – Fanon's thinking.

This does not necessarily free us from the obligation to try to understand the existential meaning of violence in Fanon's work.[13] But it does show why violence could play such a crucial role in his thinking. We cannot discuss the role of violence in Fanon without at the same time discussing the relevance of the reading of Hegel that made it possible, if not unavoidable.

Notes

1 On Fanon's reading of Mannoni, see chapter three by Ulrike Kistner in this book.

2 'A subject becomes self-conscious, or in Cartesian language – "certain of itself", in bringing the other under its control, in a word "only by sublating this other that presents itself to him as self-subsistent life (*selbständiges Leben*)".' (Rockmore 1997, p. 63)

3 Hegel's chapter on self-consciousness takes its starting point, as the reader will recall, in the idea that the object can no longer be outside consciousness since the latter is constituted by it.

4 For a different interpretation see Axel Honneth (2012).

5 See Pierre-Jean Labarrière (2014). For a different reading see Susan Buck-Morss (2009). Buck-Morss claims that Hegel's description of what she calls the 'master–slave' dialectic is inspired by the Haitian revolution of 1804. Her argument remains in my view entirely circumstantial, without taking into account the logic of the text itself.

6 'Thus he is the pure, essential action in this relationship …'. (Hegel [1807] 1977, p. 116 – §191)

7 'The Slave, in transforming the given World by his work, transcends the given and what is given by that given in himself; hence, he goes beyond himself, and also goes beyond the Master who is tied to the given which, not working, he leaves intact. If the fear of death, incarnated for the Slave in the person of the warlike Master, is the *sine qua non* of historical progress, it is solely the Slave's work that realizes and perfects it.' (Kojève [1947] 1980, p. 23)

8 'What he wants from the slave is not recognition but work. In the same way, the slave here is in no way identifiable with the slave who loses himself in the object and finds in his work the source of his liberation.' (Fanon [1952] 2008, p. 172 n. 8)

9   In Hegel's *Phenomenology*, the labouring consciousness – and only on the
     condition that it has experienced the fear of death, the absolute master –
     inscribes the negativity of self-consciousness into the object, so that the
     latter knows itself in the object and becomes thinking. This allows self-
     consciousness to re-establish its relation to the object. The idea that the slave-
     worker is the true subject of history as a process of continuous liberation
     only makes sense from a Kojèvian (and more generally speaking, Marxist)
     point of view. Fanon claims that this liberating role cannot take place in the
     colonial relation because of the 'alienation' of the (black) slave who wants to
     be like the (white) master. This alienation blocks the dialectical development
     (Fanon [1952] 2008, p. 178).

10   Fanon is probably thinking here of the history of slavery in Martinique.

11   However, it is not always clear whether Fanon is talking about the colonial
     system as such or only about the French colony.

12   In her famous preface to the 2002 French edition of *The Wretched of the Earth*
     (Cherki 2002), Alice Cherki rightly rejects Sartre's interpretation of the
     role of violence in Fanon. Sartre indeed seems to read Fanon as justifying
     individual murder: 'Read Fanon: you will see that in a time of helplessness,
     murderous rampage is the collective unconscious of the colonized' (Sartre
     [1961] 2004, p. lii). This is a much more radical position than that of Fanon,
     to whom Sartre's idealisation of violence did not make much sense.

13   For a reading probing the existential meaning of violence in Fanon's work,
     see the chapter by Beata Stawarska in this book.

References

Arendt, Hannah (1970). *On Violence*. Los Angeles: Harcourt Brace Jovanovich.

Buck-Morss, Susan (2009). *Hegel, Haiti, and Universal History*. Pittsburgh: University of Pittsburgh Press.

Cherki, Alice (2002). 'Préface à l'édition de 2002'. In Frantz Fanon, *Les damnés de la terre* (1961). Paris: Dévouverte/Poche.

Cobben, Paul (1996). *Post-dialectische zedelijkheid: Ontwerp voor een Hegeliaans antwoord op Heidegger, Habermas, Derrida en Levinas*. Kampen: Kok Agora.

Cruysberghs, Paul (1983). 'Het statuut van de lichamelijkheid in Hegels antropologie'. *Tijdschrift voor Filosofie* 45(4): 539–69.

Fanon, Frantz (2004). *The Wretched of the Earth* (1961). Translated by Richard Philcox. New York: Grove Press.

Fanon, Frantz (2008). *Black Skin, White Masks* (1952). Translated by Charles Lam Markmann. London: Pluto Press.

Gibson, Nigel (2003). *Fanon: The Postcolonial Imagination*. Cambridge: Polity Press.

Hegel, Georg Wilhelm Friedrich (1955). *Grundlinien der Philosophie des Rechts* (1821). Hamburg: Felix Meiner Verlag.

Hegel, Georg Wilhelm Friedrich (1977). *Hegel's Phenomenology of Spirit* (1807). Translated by A.V. Miller. Oxford: Oxford University Press.

Honneth, Axel (2012). 'From Desire to Recognition: Hegel's Grounding of Self-Consciousness'. In Axel Honneth, *The I in We: Studies in the Theory of Recognition.* Cambridge: Polity Press.

Jenkins, Scott (2009). 'Hegel's Concept of Desire'. *Journal of the History of Philosophy* 47(1): 103–30.

Kleinberg, Ethan (2003). 'Kojève and Fanon: The Desire for Recognition and the Fact of Blackness'. In Tyler Edward Stovall and Georges Van Den Abbeele (eds), *French Civilisation and its Discontents: Nationalism, Colonialism, Race.* New York and Oxford: New Lexington Books.

Kojève, Alexandre (1980). *Introduction to the Reading of Hegel: Lectures on the Phenomenology of Spirit* (1947). Assembled by Raymond Queneau, edited by Allan Bloom, translated by James H. Nichols Jr. Ithaca: Cornell University Press.

Labarrière, Pierre-Jean (2014). *Hegel: La phénoménologie de l'esprit.* Paris: Ellipses.

Rockmore, Tom (1997). *Cognition: An Introduction to Hegel's Phenomenology of Spirit.* Los Angeles: University of California Press.

Sartre, Jean-Paul (2004). 'Preface' (1961). In Frantz Fanon, *The Wretched of the Earth.* Translated by Richard Philcox. New York: Grove Press.

3 | Reading Hegel's *Gestalten* – Beyond Coloniality

Ulrike Kistner

In the wake of the 'decolonial turn', Georg Wilhelm Friedrich Hegel's *Phenomenology of Spirit* (Hegel [1807] 1977) has made a comeback into philosophy curricula that would be inexplicable if it were not for its much-quoted 'master–slave dialectic'. The configuration thus named relies on a particular interpretation (by Alexandre Kojève in the 1930s) and translation (into French by Jean Hyppolite in 1939–1942) of Hegel's terms '*Herr*' and '*Knecht*' as '*maître*' and '*esclave*', respectively, that have shaped the French and transatlantic reception of Hegel's work ever since (Hyppolite [1947] 1974; Kojève [1947] 1980). This is the translation that has become entrenched in common parlance, with accounts of Hegel's figural dialectics moving all the way through the knowledge chain – from Hegel via Kojève and Hyppolite to Jean-Paul Sartre (despite the fact that Hyppolite and Sartre did not directly attend Kojève's lectures; see Arthur 1983), Frantz Fanon, Jacques Lacan, Slavoj Žižek, and latter-day Africana phenomenology and existentialism, right down to Wikipedia entries and Spark Notes on Hegel[1] – and, not least, into our own teaching of post-Enlightenment history of philosophy over the years.[2]

Kojève's and Hyppolite's interpretation and translation of Hegel's *Phenomenology*, and the ensuing reception, proved formative, in turn, for engagements in the ambit of the French academy under the impact of anticolonial struggles, including those of Jean-Paul Sartre – particularly Sartre's 1961 Preface to Fanon's *Les damnés de la terre* (Sartre 1961) – and Frantz Fanon, and since then for Africana phenomenology and Africana existentialism. They have more recently received renewed impetus from Susan Buck-Morss's eminently undergraduate-teachable work on 'Hegel and Haiti' (Buck-Morss 2000, 2009), which insists that Hegel cannot be thought (and taught) without Haiti (2009, p. 16); it suggests that neglect of Haitian history would be tantamount to complicity in the exclusion of the colonial experience from Western thought (2009, pp. 16–19).

In reviewing Buck-Morss's book, *Hegel, Haiti, and Universal History* (2009), David Scott – who can hardly be accused of ignoring or occluding Haitian history – casts doubt on Buck-Morss's conjecture. How is it possible, Scott asks, to stipulate Hegel's reading about the events of the Haitian slave uprising on the pages of the journal *Minerva* as evidence for the conception of the figures of lordship and bondage in the *Phenomenology* (Scott 2010, p. 157)? He elaborates the question by asking:

> … can it be shown that New World slavery and the Haitian Revolution that overthrew one instance of it constituted *a* – if not *the* – generative problem-space out of which the *Phenomenology* was conceived and written? What would be required to demonstrate this? And second, does the conceptual relation between lordship and bondage in Hegel's discussion of self-consciousness answer a question in some relevant sense posed by the cognitive-historical problem of New World slavery and its revolutionary overthrow? And again, what sort of historical and conceptual work would be required to show that this is so? (2010, p. 157)

Indeed, there is much more conclusive evidence of what Hegel actually read – which entirely escapes Buck-Morss's reading of Hegel. Of course, Hegel read the Presocratics (Heraclitus and Anaxagoras in particular), Plato, Aristotle, Plotinus, Jakob Böhme, René Descartes and Jean-Jacques Rousseau; and he read his contemporaries, with whom he stood in intense and at times acrimonious debate – Immanuel Kant, Gotthold Ephraim Lessing, Johann Wolfgang von Goethe, Johann Fichte, Friedrich Schelling and Friedrich Hölderlin. There is one source, moreover, that just cannot be missed, as Hegel cites his work repeatedly, and in different contexts, namely Denis Diderot; and he is the only one granted the honour of being cited directly in Hegel's *Phenomenology*.[3]

This is what I will undertake in this chapter: to read Hegel reading – and reading this source in particular. More particularly, I want to ask whether and how this reading figures in relation to the colonial encounter, where it links up with the antagonistic exchange between Frantz Fanon and Octave Mannoni on the 'Psychology of Colonization' (Fanon [1952] 1986, pp. 83–108; Mannoni [1950] 1990).

But I am jumping ahead of myself.

Hegel's 'shapes of consciousness'

Let me start where my fellow travellers in drawing out the trajectories between Hegel and Fanon have left off. I would like to take up David Scott's doubt (Scott 2010, p. 157), and Philippe Van Haute's more explicit argument in his chapter in this book, that render Kojève's translation of '*Herr*' and '*Knecht*' as 'master' and 'slave', respectively, and its application to the colonial relation between master and slave, fundamentally questionable. To elaborate: Hegel himself explicitly asserts a distinction between the concepts '*Sklave/Sklaverei*' and '*Knecht/Knechtschaft*'. These terms feature differently in his different works: in the *System of Ethical Life* (Hegel [1802–1804] 1979b) as 'slavery'; in the *Phenomenology* ([1807] 1977) as 'lordship and bondage'; in the *Philosophy of Right* ([1821] 1967a) as 'slavery'; and in the Introduction to *The Philosophy of History* ([1837] 2001) as 'slavery'.[4]

What is clear in Hegel's conceptualisation of 'Self-Consciousness' (chapter IV in the *Phenomenology*), is that lord and bondsman are not anthropomorphic figures, but 'two opposed shapes of consciousness

(*Gestalten des Bewusstseins*)' (Hegel [1807] 1977, p. 115 – §189) at the initial stage of a developmental trajectory towards self-consciousness – that 'spiritual odyssey' that describes Hegel's *Phenomenology* (Arthur 1983).[5] What is also clear is that the dialectic between a spontaneous sense of freedom and a universal form of freedom unfolds in the course of a struggle that results in the antagonistic positions of lord and bondsman – which would not be accessible to the slave, since the slave is constituted as an object, a possession. The exclusion of the (historical) figure of the slave from the very possibility of coming into self-consciousness, as consciousness for-itself, is also evident in Hegel's contention that ancient slaves were not included in the definition of 'man' (Hegel [1821] 1967a, p. 15);[6] they could therefore, in his account, not be said to achieve universal self-consciousness (see Cole 2014, pp. 71–72). Where Hegel does explicitly mention slavery, it is with reference to Africa (in the Introduction to the *Philosophy of History*; see Hegel [1837] 2001, pp. 110–117) and to the ancient world, particularly as it features in Roman law (in the *Philosophy of Right*; see Hegel [1821] 1967a, pp. 15, 39).

There are thus grounds for agreeing with Philippe Van Haute's argument, in his chapter in this book, that in the *Phenomenology*, 'Hegel is not describing a real or historical situation, let alone slavery as it existed in his day', and that 'Hegel's perspective … is primarily epistemological and ontological, not socio-political'. The epistemological-ontological perspective is mediated through 'shapes of consciousness'. Consciousness itself assumes a *Gestalt* structure that formally corresponds to abstract concepts of philosophical reflection. In the footsteps of Goethe, Hegel is concerned to give 'an adequate representation', in tying 'characters to historical figures' (see Hulbert 1983, pp. 273, 274), and rather homologically so. Casting pre-theoretical 'ordinary' consciousness into concrete *Gestalten des Bewusstseins*, Hegel develops a cast of *personae* that spans the breadth of the historical development of human activity, epistemology and ontology.

Looking for the context of Hegel's *Gestalten* of lord and bondsman in the most basic forms of the 'independence' and 'dependence' of self-consciousness (of chapter IV A), respectively, many historical-critical readers of Hegel have found it in the historical figures of European medieval feudal relations (Adorno [1970] 1997, p. 345; Cole 2014, pp. 67, 69; see also Germana 2017, p. 101).

Hegel's 'bondage'

In the *Phenomenology*, we find three types of 'bondage' in the development of self-consciousness.

The first type – which is the subject of the much-vaunted master–slave dialectic – appears in the relatively undeveloped and abstract forms of independent ('being-for-self' as an other to the bondsman) and dependent (translated as 'servile', 'subservient' by A.V. Miller [Hegel (1807) 1977]) self-consciousness (non-reflexive 'being-for-self') in chapter IV, 'Self-Consciousness – The Truth of Self-Certainty'. It is through fear and 'service' (*Dienst*) that consciousness of itself becomes formed as consciousness for-itself. Without countering fear and entering service in the process of the formative activity (*'Bilden/Formieren'*), Hegel says, 'having a "mind of one's own" (*Eigensinn*) is self-will, a freedom which is still enmeshed in servitude (*Knechtschaft*)' ([1807] 1977, pp. 118–19 – §196). Thus, we have here three modes of serfdom:

- subservient, dependent self-consciousness (*'Unselbständigkeit des Selbstbewusstseins'*);
- service (*'Dienst'*) – 'the serving/servile consciousness' in Terry Pinkard and Michael Baur's translation of *'das dienende Bewusstsein'* (Hegel [1807] 2018) – in the process of the formative activity (*'Bilden'*) of becoming for-itself;
- servitude (*'Knechtschaft'*, translated by Pinkard and Baur as 'servility') – as a form of self-will (*'Eigensinn'*), undifferentiated from itself (Hegel [1807] 1977, pp. 118–21 – §§196, 197).

A second type of 'bondage' in Hegel's text features only obliquely, implicitly. In chapter VI, 'servility' can no longer be discerned as a distinct position of self-consciousness. Systematic self-reflection passes over into 'shapes of a world' ('*Gestalten einer Welt*') (Hegel [1807] 1977, p. 265 – §441), formed through 'ethical life' ('*Sittlichkeit*'), 'enculturation' ('*Bildung*') and 'morality' ('*Moralität*'). A third variation on the theme of bondage, one which breaks through the bounds of bondage, will be discussed in what follows, in tracking further transmutations of Hegel's *Gestalten*.

In section B I.a of the chapter entitled 'The World of Self-Alienated Spirit', 'Culture and its Realm of Actuality' (chapter VI B I.a), too, we learn about the alienation of spirit in the process of enculturation (*Bildung*) in the revolutionising consciousness of the Enlightenment (Hegel [1807] 1977, p. 265 – §442; see also p. 296 – §486). The 'culture' of 'universal talk', as Hegel calls it ([1807] 1977, pp. 316–17 – §521), corresponds to the rediscovery of dialogue in literary and philosophical discourse in the Enlightenment, 'at the moment when the dialectic consciously emerges' (Lukács [1966] 1975, p. 495). Within this culture, Hegel situates what he deems the most highly developed freedom of self-consciousness.

Yet in this culture, the actual world and the world of thought are inverted: notions of good and bad, noble and ignoble consciousness are reversed, changing into each other, in and through the interchange of dialogue:

> It exists in the universal talk and destructive judgement which strips of their significance all those moments which are supposed to count as the true being and as actual members of the whole, and is equally this nihilistic game which it plays with itself. This judging and talking is, therefore, what is true and invincible, while it overpowers everything; it is solely with this alone that one has truly to do with in this actual world. In this world, the Spirit of each part finds expression, or is wittily talked about, and finds said about it what it is. (Hegel [1807] 1977, p. 317 – §521)

Enter Diderot's *Rameau's Nephew*

At this point, the narrator of Diderot's *Rameau's Nephew* enters the fray, quoted in three instances disrupting Hegel's discourse itself (without mention of Diderot as the source).[7] In Diderot's text, the role of a master, associated with mastery of musical form, technique and performance, is written out of the dialogue, while its shadow looms large: it is that of composer, theorist of harmony and *virtuoso* musician Jean-Philippe Rameau.[8] Instead, the Nephew, Jean-François Rameau, piano teacher and improvising violinist, emerges as the prominent figure. Yet the Nephew is an epigone: he can only aspire to the virtuosity of his uncle, the Master-composer/musician, 'the great Rameau' (Diderot [1823] 1986b, p. 48), whom he jealously impersonates (pp. 43, 44).

The reflexively disrupted consciousness (Hegel [1807] 1977, pp. 320–21 – §526) of '*Lui*', variously associated with the Nephew in the dialogue of Diderot's text, attains in Hegel's text the role of giving voice, in 'self-conscious eloquence of the educated mind', to 'universal deception'. Through the casting of the interlocution in the divided roles – not between the first and the second person, but between the first person '*Moi*' (the moot philosophical voice) and the third person '*Lui*' (the versatile voice enacting a plurality of other voices) – Diderot's text breaks the framework of the dialogue to create a literary heterologue. Hegel finds *Lui*'s speech risibly and vainly inverting, in 'witty talk' ([1807] 1977, p. 320 – §526), what is held to be 'noble' and 'good'; *Lui*'s speech finds its truth ([1807] 1977, pp. 320–21 – §526) in that inversion – 'in making the opposite of the noble and good into the condition and necessity of the noble and good' ([1807] 1977, p. 319 – §523). Hegel's self-disrupted consciousness, instantiated in *Lui* in Diderot's text, can occupy all positions, including their reverse, and yet no single one; it is the consciousness of the contamination of all opposites in and by each other (see Gearhart 1986, p. 1050), and the reversal of standpoints, dissolving their antithesis.

Hegel's citation of Diderot's text most closely tracks the position of *Lui*, the position of the Nephew, who 'triumphs not so much through the game of question-and-answer as through the genius of his pantomime, by means of which he relinquishes his individuality in the unbounded plurality of "alien voices"'(Jauss 1983, p. 11).

However, Hegel's reading of Diderot's dialogical text superimposes itself on the narrator of *Rameau's Nephew* in a kind of voice-over through which the characters become unified and legible as forms of consciousness typifying *Geist*-historical figures.[9] Thus, Hegel's reading evens out Diderot's jagged contestatory text, and assimilates it to his own project (see Hulbert 1983, p. 284).

'Bondage' recast: Hegel's and Diderot's valet

A third variation on the theme of 'bondage', in addition to the two discussed above, appears in chapter VI C.c, 'Conscience. The "Beautiful Soul", Evil and its Forgiveness'. It is this variation that is of interest to me in exploring the debate between Fanon and Mannoni, with reference to their different readings of Hegel's *Phenomenology*. Here Hegel once again turns to the 'universal talk and destructive judgement' which he sees at work in Enlightenment culture, and which he had earlier in the *Phenomenology* described through the irruption of Diderot's dialogical *Rameau's Nephew* (Diderot [1823] 1986b). In chapter VI C.c, the figure of the servant – the valet (*Kammerdiener*), to be precise – is invoked in an antagonistic relationship to the figure acting, analogous to the relationship of an individual, partial perspective to the universal perspective of concrete action (Hegel [1807] 1977, pp. 403–404 – §665). In creating this analogy, Hegel adduces the witticism attributed to Madame de Cornuel:[10] 'No man is a hero to his valet; not, however, because the man is not a hero, but because the valet – is a valet, whose dealings are with the man, not as a hero, but as one who eats, drinks, and wears clothes, in general, with his individual wants and fancies' ([1807] 1977, p. 404 – §665).

Returning to the relation between judgement and action, which the relation between the valet and the master is supposed to demonstrate by analogy, Hegel explains that for the judging consciousness (personified in the valet), there is no action in which it could not oppose to the universal aspect of the action (personified in the hero, who is not the hero – for either self or other) the personal aspect of the individuality, and thus play the part of the moral valet towards the agent ([1807] 1977, p. 404 – §665).

For the unfolding antagonistic dialogical interchange between the valet (the judging consciousness) and the acting consciousness in Hegel's chapter VI C.c, Diderot's *Jacques the Fatalist and His Master* (written between 1765 and 1780, and published in 1796) provides the template, but this time without quotation marks and once again without reference to its source (Diderot [1796] 1986a).

Diderot's text is constructed as a playful dialogue in the form of a Menippean satire that overflows any determinate genre delimitations and styles, and any fixed points of view, between a Master who is continuously in the process of losing his mastery – and indeed, the plot – and the insolent valet who is his valet not by personal dependency, but by the axis of their interlocutions, itself constantly shifting.[11] In that respect, there are some parallels to be drawn with *Rameau's Nephew*, as discussed above. But, with *Jacques the Fatalist*, there are some twists, no less consequential for Hegel's scheme. In *Jacques the Fatalist*, the Master is not named, nor is he endowed with personalised attributes. And the possessive pronoun of the title *Jacques ... and His Master* is ironically deceptive: the Master, as it turns out, is not Jacques's (or anyone's) master. Jacques, appearing both in name and epithet, triumphs – not through labour, but through his wit. He attains mastery over things, without aspiring to the title of Master. He instructs the so-called master that it is futile for the latter, in his turn, to slip into the position of the valet; he would only lose his title, without attaining mastery over things.

Hegel's 'judging consciousness' – personified in the valet – is base and hypocritical, setting itself up as knowledge superior to the action – personified in the hero – that it discredits. The judging consciousness sets itself up on the same level as the action on which it passes judgement. The acting consciousness thus recognises the judging consciousness as the same as itself. The acting consciousness confesses this to the judging consciousness, and envisages a reciprocal move from the judging consciousness, in the expectation of mutual recognition (Hegel [1807] 1977, p. 405 – §666). But the judging consciousness denies the acting consciousness the possibility of mutual recognition. In doing so, it repulses the acting consciousness that made the confession. The judging consciousness keeps itself to itself, 'retain[ing] within itself and for itself its uncommunicative being-for-self'. In doing so, it fails to attain objective existence, actual Spirit: '[it] itself has the certainty of its Spirit, not in an actual deed, but in its inner being, and finds the outer existence of this inner being in the *utterance* of its judgement' ([1807] 1977, p. 406 – §667). It remains in the 'unreconciled immediacy' that Hegel also calls 'madness' (*'zur Verrücktheit zerrüttet'*) – the madness that characterises the 'beautiful soul' ([1807] 1977, pp. 406–407 – §668). It is only when the judging consciousness forgives the other (that is, the acting consciousness) and renounces itself as unreal being, and when it 'acknowledges that what thought characterized as bad, viz. action, is good' ([1807] 1977, p. 408 – §670) that reciprocal recognition is possible. At this point, the Hegelian synthesis closes the chapter.

Before moving on from this discussion of Hegel's reading of Diderot's characters, I would like to return, for a moment, to the figure of the valet in relation to the hero. Much as Hegel lends a *persona* to the judging consciousness – the valet – he remains within the idiom of the French proverb. Similarly to Jacques's master in Diderot's text, Hegel's acting consciousness is hardly personified. The other who is *not* the hero of the valet is neither master nor lord, nor any other category borrowed from the feudal social or political hierarchy. The other of the valet has receded. Still, the figure of the valet (*Kammerdiener*) denotes a form of intimate personal servitude that, in Hegel's scheme, holds the power of forgiveness, and therefore the key to reciprocal recognition.

Fanon and Mannoni in and on the colonial encounter

Much as we might be tempted to see Hegel's 'Spirit' moving in constellations corresponding to social and political formations from feudalism through the Enlightenment to revolution, and thus pertaining exclusively to European rationality,[12] this becomes questionable if we see this movement not only through a Fanonian lens, but through the debate (another antagonistic dialogue) between Fanon, writing from the experience of post-slavery society in Martinique in 1952, and Mannoni, writing from Madagascar at the time of the Malagasy Uprising (1944–47).

The social divisions opening up in the colonial encounter are attributed by Mannoni to colonial modernity. They arise, he suggests, with the political-social-cultural-psychic injunction for the subject to become independent from parental and primary group ties (while incurring guilt in the process). In the colonial situation, this injunction is imposed on a precolonial *feudal* subject interpellated in a socio-cultural-psychically integral form of dependency, which tends to become a 'complex' only in the course of its dislodging in the colonial encounter.

For Fanon, on the other hand, the conflictual colonial encounter pivots centrally on *race*: 'The first encounter with a white man oppresses [the Negro] with the whole weight of his blackness' (Fanon [1952] 1986, p. 143). The lines of division are drawn – and drawn racially – with colonial oppression: 'The Negro is in every sense of the word a victim of white civilisation – whether as slave of a cultural imposition, or, identifying with the white man, as slave of himself' ([1952] 1986, p. 192).

The preoccupation with the construction of contrary and mutually exclusive personality types structured by inferiority and dependence (see Mannoni [1950] 1990, p. 41) was what raised Fanon's and Césaire's hackles about Mannoni's project. To be sure, Mannoni's culturalist-psychological account of the colonial encounter was premised on, and in turn generated, expansive historical and political blindspots (see Bloch 1990, pp. v, vi). Yet Mannoni retains a historical perspective in relation to broadly differentiated modes of socio-cultural-psychic structuration. He notes the colonially engendered 'dependency complex' in particularly pronounced forms in the case of strong vertical ties corresponding to feudalism. This description, Mannoni finds, fits the Merina ([1950] 1990, p. 41), who historically occupied the central highlands of the island known today as Madagascar, and consolidated their polities into a kingdom towards the end of the eighteenth century.

For the inhabitants of the coastal regions of Madagascar with historical links to the East African coast, on the other hand, 'dependency' does not emerge as a complex in the colonial encounter in quite the same way; in this case, it is inflected by horizontal, egalitarian networks (see Bloch 1990, p. ix; Mannoni [1950] 1990, p. 66).

Thus, despite the fact that Mannoni's analysis of subjectivities in colonial conflict does not stand up to empirical-historical and ethnographic-methodological scrutiny, his differentiation of modes of psycho-social organisation is of some interest, which I would like to spell out further.

The so-called dependency complex of Mannoni's 'psychology of colonization' in Madagascar is predicated on a precolonial social matrix characterised by a history of trans-oceanic Austronesian and African migration and settlement, internal conquest and slave-trading, sovereign dominions, feudal hierarchies and central state formation – which he clearly distinguishes from the social de-structuration in the French slave colonies. Under a system of rule implanted on a history of colonial slavery, Mannoni avers, 'assimilation' is the more likely scenario, as 'the personality of the native is first destroyed through uprooting, enslavement, and the collapse of the social structure' ([1950] 1990, p. 27). This pertains to 'the older colonies' that, as the translator explains, 'remained after the eighteenth century and had been based on slavery – such as the Antilles and Réunion' (Mannoni [1950] 1990, p. 27 n. 1). Thus, despite the fact that Mannoni does not explicitly refer to Hegel's *personae* of lord and bondsman in his *Psychology of Colonization*, he specifies for his investigation a form of colonialism implanted upon feudal relations.

On the differentiation between trans-oceanic slavery and colonialism, modes of subjugation and modes of subjection, which Mannoni elaborates, Fanon is compelled to concede some ground. Not all forms of rule over 'the black man' are based on a history of slavery; and not all subjects emerging 'out of slavery' are interpellated as turning their enslavement onto themselves. Fanon quotes Gabriel d'Arbousier's critique of Sartre and *négritude* in this context:

> When Sartre wrote, 'Simply by plunging into the depths of his memory as a former slave, the black man asserts that suffering is the lot of man and that it is no less undeserved on that account,' did he take into consideration what that might mean for a Hova,[13] a Moor, a Touareg, a Peul, or a Bantu of the Congo or the Ivory Coast? (Fanon [1952] 1986, p. 172)

Fanon's 'slave' and Mannoni's 'valet'

Fanon admits to the lack of historical and geopolitical differentiation in his own analysis of colonial pathogeny. Writing on Martinique, he sees this pathogeny as 'the consequence of replacement of the repressed [African] spirit in the consciousness of the slave by an authority symbol representing the Master' (Fanon [1952] 1986, p. 145). Fanon here approvingly cites René Ménil's Hegelianism (Ménil 1981) in explaining the defensive reaction of a Negro intellectual. It is, he explains, his adherence to Hegelianism that drives his analysis, rather than his attention to the specific conditions of post-slavery societies of the Antilles.[14] So, by his own admission, he retains some aspects of the 'master–slave dialectic' of Hegel's chapter IV on 'Self-Consciousness' in its symbolic dimensions.

Mannoni, for his part, attests to a close reading of Hegel in the 'psychology of decolonisation' articulated in his article entitled 'The Decolonisation of Myself' (Mannoni 1966), in which he revisits his *Psychology of Colonization* twenty years after initially putting pen to paper on this subject. Mannoni's own moves, in 'The Decolonisation of Myself', closely track those of Hegel's valet in chapter VI of the *Phenomenology* – but minus Hegel's synthesis. To recall, the trajectory of Hegel's reading of Diderot's valet, as judging consciousness, is to set itself up in equivalence to the acting consciousness, which in turn seeks to enter into a relation of mutual recognition with the valet – the judging consciousness; but the valet, the judging consciousness, foils this bid by the acting consciousness.[15] No longer beholden to Hegel's chapter IV on 'Self-Consciousness', yet following Hegel's analogy of the relation between judging and acting consciousness with the relation between (Diderot's) valet and hero, Mannoni extends the role assigned by Hegel to the valet. He adduces the role of valets in the *commedia dell'arte* specifically (with whom he associates the role of the psychologist), but only to disavow it, in cautioning against installing the valet in the service of a *faux* reconciliation (Mannoni 1966, p. 331).[16]

What is in question here, I would argue, is not so much the traversal of feudalism by the culture of the European Enlightenment (after all, there are non-European forms of feudalism), as the Hegelian synthesis – that universalist solution of which Mannoni says that it 'has lost sight of the terms of the problem' (1966, p. 331). 'The Decolonisation of Myself' re-opens 'the unity of the self', 'the universal knowledge of itself', and the 'certainty of itself' of Hegel's reconciliation (Hegel [1807] 1977, p. 409 – §671). By the same token, it returns Diderot's dialogical-dialectical interlocutors to the scenario prematurely closed by Hegel's adequating voice-over.

Thus, I would want to argue that, much as the casting of Hegel's chapter IV on 'Self-Consciousness' in terms of a colonial master–slave configuration proves a dead-end for analysis of (post-)slavery sociality (as Fanon, and with him Philippe Van Haute, in his chapter in this book, have pointed out), the literary imagination at work in Hegel's *Phenomenology of Spirit* does not entirely share in this lost cause, to the extent that it engages us in a writerly reading, activating the reader as producer of the text (Barthes [1973] 1992, pp. 5–6). The dynamic set in motion with Hegel's reading of Diderot inflected his own *Gestalten* to the point of shaking the plot of the *Phenomenology*. Fanon's contestatory reading of the French Hegel, in turn, confronts Mannoni's reading of Hegel reading Diderot, in a debate through which the terms of the problem can be stated differently – as reaching beyond coloniality.

Notes

1   See Wikipedia, 'Master–slave dialectic', *Wikipedia*, viewed 21 December 2019, https://en.wikipedia.org/wiki/Master%E2%80%93slave_dialectic; SparkNotes, 'Themes, Arguments, and Ideas: Dialectic as the Fundamental Pattern of Thought', *SparkNotes*, viewed 21 December 2019, https://www.sparknotes.com/philosophy/hegel/themes/.

2   This is despite the fact that the first English translation by James Black Baillie (Hegel [1807] 1967b), and the subsequent ones by A.V. Miller (1977) and Terry Pinkard and Michael Baur (2018), do not render Hegel's '*Knecht*' as 'slave', but as 'bondsman'.

3   According to James Hulbert, there are eight instances throughout Hegel's *Collected Works* in which Diderot is mentioned – in three extended passages in the *Phenomenology*, and in two instances in the *Philosophy of History* (Hulbert 1983, pp. 272, 274).

4   See for instance Hegel's Berlin lecture on '*Herrschaft und Knechtschaft*' (Hegel 1979a, pp. 342–43).

5   In Arthur's words, '[the] *Phenomenology* is a spiritual odyssey, or perhaps, a *Bildungsroman* of spirit in which spirit discovers that the objective shapes given to it in consciousness and self-consciousness are nothing but its own self-determination' (1983, p. 71).

6   Hegel explains: 'in Roman law … there could be no definition of "man", since "slave" could not be brought under it – the very status of slave indeed is an outrage on the conception of man' ([1821] 1967a, p. 15 – §2); 'from the point of view of what is called *jus ad personam* in Roman law, a man is reckoned a person only when he is treated as possessing a certain status. Hence in Roman law, even personality itself is only a certain standing or status contrasted with slavery' ([1821] 1967a, p. 48 – §57).

7   Hegel relied on Goethe's 1805 translation of one of four copies of Diderot's manuscript in circulation in France, Russia and Germany between 1773 and 1891, namely that in the hands of Friedrich Melchior Baron von Grimm, Diderot's erstwhile friend, who distributed the text in Germany long before it appeared in print in France.

8   As a historical figure, Jean-Philippe Rameau was an exponent of French baroque opera in the tradition of Jean-Baptiste Lully, composer, musician and performer at the court of Louis XIV.

9   The interlocutions move between *Moi* as tranquil, simple consciousness, speaking for the excellent, the good, and the noble enduring unchangeably (Hulbert 1983, p. 287), and *Lui* as inconsistent 'rigmarole of wisdom and folly' (Hegel [1807] 1977, p. 318 – §522) that Hegel privileges in characterising the philosophical discourse of his time.

10   This witticism has become proverbial in French. It was attributed to Madame Anne Marie Bigot de Cornuel (1605–94) by Charlotte Aïssé (1693–1733), a celebrity in early eighteenth-century France, in one of her letters (dated 13 August 1728), which were edited by Voltaire and published in 1787 (Aïssé 1787, p. 114).

11   The role of the valet in the theatre – and Diderot's text approximates a theatrical script – is, like or even more than Hegel's other *personae*, a historical character; he 'embodies the social relationships of a specific period, and becomes the barometer and the figurehead of that period' (Pavis 1998, p. 430). 'The epitome of the popular character, the valet embodies all the contradictions of society' (1998, p. 430). Moreover, historically and in the poetics of the genre, the valet – who as a social subordinate has a superior understanding of communicative situations involving the masters – plays the role of evaluating 'the very manner in which people speak to each other and how much the social order has to do with the fact of speaking and its interpretation' (Rancière [1995] 1999, p. 48; see also p. 49); he disputes the assumption of a common understanding.

12   See also Georg Lukács's even more specific contention, drawing attention to Diderot as an important source for Hegel's *Phenomenology*, that 'from the collapse of feudalism to the French Revolution the *Phenomenology* does not leave French soil': 'Hegel shows how once-independent vassals degenerate into sycophantic courtiers and how the "noble consciousness" of the feudal lords ... had been translated into mere flattery of the monarch ... what we have here ... is the gradual bourgeoisification of absolute monarchy' (Lukács [1966] 1975, p. 491).

13   Precolonially, the Hova were free commoners, mostly merchants and farmers, erstwhile conquerors and slave-holders within the Merina kingdom, socially situated as the middle caste between Andriana nobility and Andevo slaves.

14   Fanon continues from the critique by d'Arbousier that he quotes: '[d'Arbousier's] objection is valid. It applies to me as well. In the beginning I wanted to confine myself to the Antilles. But, regardless of consequences, the dialectic took the upper hand and I was compelled to *see* that the Antillean is first of all a Negro' (Fanon [1952] 1986, p. 192).

15 See for instance Mannoni's injunction: '[No one] will assert that all the problems encountered in the actual world are due only to misunderstandings, strong
emotions, illusions; or that, once he is free of racist feelings, the white man will
be able to greet the black man as his true brother' (Mannoni 1966, p. 331).

16 In Mannoni's caustically aporetic words, '[thus] the psychologist runs the
risk of unintentionally playing the role of those valets in the *Commedia
dell'arte*, who act as go-betweens for their quarrelling masters and suc-
ceed in reconciling them up to the very moment when the masters themselves discover the true cause of their quarrel from a private conversation'
(1966, p. 331).

References

Adorno, Theodor W. (1997). *Aesthetic Theory* (1970). Edited and translated by
Robert Hullot-Kentor. Minneapolis: University of Minnesota Press.

Aïssé, Charlotte (1787). 'Lettre XIII, Août 1728'. In Voltaire (ed.), *Lettres de
Mademoiselle Aïssé a Madame Calandrini*. Paris: La Grange.

Arthur, Chris (1983). 'Hegel's master/slave dialectic and a myth of Marxology'.
New Left Review 1(142): 67–75, viewed 10 January 2020, https://www.marx-
ists.org/subject/marxmyths/chris-arthur/article.htm.

Barthes, Roland (1992). *S/Z* (1973). Translated by Richard Miller. Oxford, UK and
Cambridge, Mass.: Blackwell.

Bloch, Maurice (1990). 'New Foreword'. In Octave Mannoni, *Prospero and Caliban:
The Psychology of Colonization*. Translated by Pamela Powesland. Ann Arbor:
University of Michigan Press.

Buck-Morss, Susan (2000). 'Hegel and Haiti'. *Critical Inquiry* 26(4): 821–65.

Buck-Morss, Susan (2009). *Hegel, Haiti, and Universal History*. Pittsburgh:
University of Pittsburgh Press.

Cole, Andrew (2014). *The Birth of Theory*. Chicago and London: University of
Chicago Press.

Diderot, Denis (1986a). *Jacques the Fatalist and His Master* (1796). Translated by
Martin Henry. Harmondsworth: Penguin.

Diderot, Denis (1986b). *Rameau's Nephew* (1823). Translated by Leonard Tancock.
Harmondsworth: Penguin.

Fanon, Frantz (1986). *Black Skin, White Masks* (1952). Translated by Charles Lam
Markmann. London: Pluto Press.

Fanon, Frantz (2004). *The Wretched of the Earth* (1961). Translated by Richard
Philcox. New York: Grove Press.

Gearhart, Suzanne (1986). 'The dialectic and its aesthetic Other: Hegel and
Diderot'. *MLN* 101(5): 1042–66.

Germana, Nicholas (2017). 'Revisiting "Hegel and Haiti": Postcolonial readings of the lord/bondsman dialectic'. In Michael Monahan (ed.), *Creolizing Hegel*. London and New York: Rowman and Littlefield.

Hegel, Georg Wilhelm Friedrich (1967a). *Hegel's Philosophy of Right* (1821). Translated by Thomas Malcolm Knox. Oxford: Oxford University Press.

Hegel, Georg Wilhelm Friedrich (1967b). *The Phenomenology of Mind* (1807). Translated by James Black Baillie. London and New York: Harper and Row.

Hegel, Georg Wilhelm Friedrich (1977). *Hegel's Phenomenology of Spirit* (1807). Translated by A.V. Miller. Oxford: Clarendon Press.

Hegel, Georg Wilhelm Friedrich (1979a). *'Herrschaft und Knechtschaft'*. In Michael John Petry (ed.), *Hegel's Philosophy of Subjective Spirit*, vol. 3. Netherlands: Springer.

Hegel, Georg Wilhelm Friedrich (1979b). *System of Ethical Life* (1802/3) and 'First Philosophy of Spirit' (Part III of the *System of Speculative Philosophy* 1803/4). Edited and translated by Thomas Malcolm Knox. Albany: State University of New York Press.

Hegel, Georg Wilhelm Friedrich (2001). *The Philosophy of History* (1837). Translated by John Sibree. Kitchener, Ontario: Batoche.

Hegel, Georg Wilhelm Friedrich (2018). *The Phenomenology of Spirit* (1807). Translated by Terry Pinkard and Michael Baur. Cambridge: Cambridge University Press.

Hulbert, James (1983). 'Diderot in the text of Hegel: A question of intertextuality'. *Studies in Romanticism* 22(2): 267–91.

Hyppolite, Jean (1974). *Genesis and Structure of Hegel's Phenomenology of Spirit* (1947). Translated by Samuel Cherniak and John Heckman. Evanston: Northwestern University Press.

Jauss, Hans Robert (1983). 'The dialogical and the dialectical *Neveu de Rameau*: How Diderot adopted Socrates and Hegel adopted Diderot'. Translated by Sara Brewer Berlowitz, edited by William R. Herzog. In Centre for Hermeneutical Studies in Hellenistic and Modern Culture, *Protocol of the Forty-Fifth Colloquy*. Berkeley: University of California.

Kojève, Alexandre (1980). *Introduction to the Reading of Hegel: Lectures on the Phenomenology of Spirit* (1947). Assembled by Raymond Queneau, edited by Allan Bloom, translated by James H. Nichols Jr. Ithaca: Cornell University Press.

Lukács, Georg (1975). *The Young Hegel. Studies in the Relations between Dialectics and Economics* (1966). Translated by Rodney Livingstone. London: Merlin Press.

Mannoni, Octave (1966). 'The decolonisation of myself'. *Race* 7(4): 327–35.

Mannoni, Octave (1990). *Prospero and Caliban: The Psychology of Colonization* (1950). Translated by Pamela Powesland. Ann Arbor: University of Michigan Press.

Ménil, René (1981). *Tracées: Identité, négritude, esthétique dans l'Antilles*. Paris: Éditions Robert Laffont.

Pavis, Patrice (1998). *Dictionary of the Theatre: Terms, Concepts, and Analysis*. Translated by Christine Schantz. Toronto and Buffalo: University of Toronto Press.

Rancière, Jacques (1999). *Disagreement: Politics and Philosophy* (1995). Translated by Julie Rose. Minneapolis and London: University of Minnesota Press.

Sartre, Jean-Paul (1961). 'Préface à l'édition de 1961'. In Frantz Fanon, *Les damnés de la terre*. Paris: Découverte Poche.

Scott, David (2010). 'Antinomies of slavery, enlightenment, and universal history'. *Small Axe* 14(3): 152–62.

4 | Hegel's Lord–Bondsman Dialectic and the African: A Critical Appraisal of Achille Mbembe's Colonial Subjects

Josias Tembo

In postcolonial theory and critical race theory, Georg Wilhelm Friedrich Hegel is (in)famously known for two things – firstly, for his lord–bondsman dialectic in the *Phenomenology of Spirit* (Hegel [1807] 1977), which has been mistranslated as the 'master–slave dialectic'; and secondly, for the racism expressed in his lectures on the *Philosophy of History* (Hegel [1837] 2001). The lord–bondsman dialectic as a struggle for spiritual unity of two aspects of a shape of self-consciousness in the *Phenomenology* has been construed in terms of the struggle of racialised and colonised African subjects in Hegel's description in the *Philosophy of History*. There has been a tendency to reference the lord–bondsman dialectic in conceptualising the process of African enslavement, colonisation and liberation, on the basis of what Hegel outlined in his lectures on the *Philosophy of History* as the consciousness of Negroes lacking self-conscious history. What concerns me here is the relationship between the shapes of self-consciousness designated in the *Phenomenology* as the lord–bondsman dialectic and the ascriptions, in the Introduction to the *Philosophy of History*, of unconsciousness and sub-humanity to indigenous people of sub-Saharan Africa, who are said to be devoid of universal historical self-consciousness. This relationship poses the question: is the self-consciousness of the lord–bondsman dialectic in the *Phenomenology* the same as the self-consciousness in world history and the self-consciousness attributed to the indigenous peoples of sub-Saharan Africa in the *Philosophy of History*? The answer to this question has implications for our understanding of Hegel's argument in the *Philosophy of History* that the indigenous people of sub-Saharan Africa lack self-conscious history, and for the philosophical understanding of African slavery, colonisation and liberation processes based on the model of the lord–bondsman dialectic.

In trying to clarify the notion of the shapes of self-consciousness in Hegel's philosophy, and the way in which this notion has been instrumentalised to theorise the processes of African slavery, colonisation and struggles for liberation, this chapter tackles three tasks. Firstly, it expounds Achille Mbembe's application of the notion of the lord–bondsman dialectic in his book *On the Postcolony* (Mbembe 2001) in explaining the processes of African slavery, colonisation and liberation. Secondly, the chapter attempts to clear away the confusion arising from the conflation of the shapes of self-consciousness engaged in the lord–bondsman dialectic with human self-consciousness. And lastly, the chapter exposes the theoretical and historical costs of this conflation for an understanding of African slavery, colonisation and liberation. This conflation, and the instrumentalisation of the lord–bondsman dialectic, produces colonial subjects without historical agency.

Mbembe's slavery/colonial subjects and Hegel's lord–bondsman dialectic

In the chapter entitled 'Out of the World' in *On the Postcolony* (2001), Mbembe considers the violence of death (the literal killing of human beings and deprivation of humanity) in the colonial encounter and the forms through which this violence was accomplished and normalised. He focuses on the violence of death as it pertains to the ways in which Africa and African subjects emerge in modern and contemporary discourse as devoid of consciousness and clarity of self-knowledge (Mbembe 2001, p. 174). [1] For Mbembe, understanding violence in the colonial encounter entails attending to the following questions: what does it mean to do violence to human beings who are considered not human? Who confers the status of humanity on some and not on other human beings, and by what authority is this qualification made? Such questions lead Mbembe to his last question: 'how do these matters relate to the birth of the subject, and the relation between freedom and bondage?' (2001, p. 174).

Engaging with Hegel's *Philosophy of History*, which he takes as a prototype for the colonial mode of constructing Africa and the African subject (2001, p. 176), Mbembe theorises the birth of the colonised subject and its relation to freedom and bondage. In presenting Hegel's ideas, he closely follows Hegel's theorisation of the consciousness of the indigenous peoples of sub-Saharan Africa (whom Hegel refers to as Negroes); in this chapter I will refer to Hegel's construal as 'Negro-consciousness'.[2] Mbembe begins by reminding us that for Hegel, sub-Saharan Africa is difficult to conceptualise: 'Hegelian discourse regards Africa – what passes for Africa – as a vast tumultuous world of drives and sensations, so tumultuous and opaque as to be practically impossible to represent, but which words must nevertheless grasp and anchor in pre-set certainty ... to describe Africa demands that the subject make the journey from sense to reason in the opposite direction' (2001, p. 176).

Engaging with Hegel's Introduction to the *Philosophy of History*, Mbembe explains that for Europeans to understand Negro-consciousness they must put aside all that is human, because the African is constituted by 'all that is foreign to man in his immediate existence, and nothing consonant with humanity is to be found in his character' (2001, p. 176 citing Hegel [1837] 2001, pp. 179–90). The condition in which Negroes live, according to Hegel, is

> incapable of any development or culture, and their present exis-
> tence is the same as it has always been. In face of the enormous
> energy of sensuous arbitrariness which dominates their lives,

morality has no determinate influence upon them. Anyone who wishes to study the most terrible manifestations of human nature will find them in Africa. The earliest reports concerning this continent tell us precisely the same, and it has no history in the true sense of the word ... What we understand as Africa proper is that unhistorical and undeveloped land which is still enmeshed in the natural spirit, and which had to be mentioned here before we cross the threshold of world history itself. (Mbembe 2001, p. 178 citing Hegel [1837] 2001, pp. 176–77)

For Hegel, 'Africa proper' (sub-Saharan Africa, in this context), as the continent of Negro-consciousness, is motionless and culturally impotent, incapable of objective and universal subjectivity and therefore incapable of world-historical existence. To frame the dehumanising violence that European thought and practices wrought on African subjects, Mbembe reads Hegel's exposition of what I call Negro-consciousness in the Introduction to the *Philosophy of History* as premised on the binary opposition of the 'I' and the 'non-I'. European consciousness belongs to the ontological condition of the 'I' (self-consciousness), while Negro-consciousness is a 'non-I' (2001, p. 190). The consciousness that makes up European self-consciousness is radically different from the consciousness that makes up Negro-consciousness. For Mbembe, in denying Africans historical self-consciousness, Hegel also denies them everything that is human.

Setting out the meaning of Hegel's ideas in the Introduction to the *Philosophy of History* and in the *Phenomenology*, Mbembe interprets Hegel's 'mental universe' with the aid of Maurice Merleau-Ponty's *Phenomenology of Perception* (Merleau-Ponty [1945] 1962). In Hegel's mental universe, and by extension in the dominant Western colonial mental universe, Mbembe states, 'there are two modes of being, and two only: being in itself, that of objects arrayed in space, and being for itself, that of consciousness' (Mbembe 2001, p. 190, citing Merleau-Ponty [1945] 1962, p. 349).[3] Accordingly, a human being exists as both being-in-itself and being-for-itself. Mbembe further argues that the status of another human being as a unity of being-in-itself (existing in space) and being-for-itself (existing as self-consciousness) has proved to be difficult to imagine in so-called objective thought (by implication Hegelian thought). He states that 'in Hegel appears the idea that affirmation of a foreign consciousness in face of mine relieves my own being of all value – and it is Hegel who pushes this idea to its extreme limits' (2001, p. 191). Here Mbembe seems to be presenting ideas from both the *Phenomenology of Spirit* and the *Philosophy of History* as contained within a single system, one which denies the self-consciousness of non-European peoples – and in this context, of the indigenous peoples of sub-Saharan Africa. Basing his analysis on both the *Phenomenology* and the Introduction to the *Philosophy of History*, Mbembe takes Hegel to be construing a single shape of self-consciousness framed by the 'I'–'non-I' opposition. Summarising what he believes to be Hegel's notion of self-consciousness in the *Phenomenology* and the *Philosophy of History*, he writes:

> ... first, Hegel's central obsession – also to be found in Nietzsche – [is] the obsession with *hierarchy* ... There is, next, the equivalence Hegel establishes among the three notions of particularity, life, and totality – three notions culminating, in his thought, in the notion of self-consciousness. Self-consciousness is that consciousness having for object and absolute essence the particular, the *I*. The *I* must be that singular entity whose peculiar feature is to posit itself to the exclusion of everything that is other. Hegel's reasoning proceeds as follows: my life is particularity; my particularity is totality; my totality is consciousness; and my consciousness is life. Self-consciousness, the knowing of itself, self-identity: all this is raised up to the status of 'native realm of truth'. Difference has no being, or, if it has, then only as the reverse of everything that I am, as error, folly – in short, the 'objective negative'. All that counts is the motionless tautology of *'I am I'*.[4] (2001, pp. 191–92)

Having exposed what he believes to be Hegel's notion of self-consciousness as expounded in the *Phenomenology*, Mbembe proceeds to offer an account of what he understands to be Hegel's notions of freedom, bondage and violence as these exist in the lord–bondsman dialectic presented later in the *Phenomenology*, arguing that they are characteristic of historical self-consciousness as presented in the *Philosophy of History*. He writes:

> There is, finally, the relationship that Hegel establishes between, on the one hand, lordship and bondage, and, on the other, violence, suicide, and freedom. We shall not consider in detail his discussion of the relationship between master and slave. That discussion can be summarized as concerned with a central theme: self-consciousness in relation to another self-consciousness. The destiny of that relation plays out around a particular moment, the moment of *recognition*. Without recognition, each of the two self-consciousnesses, exposed to one another in immediate face-to-face, naturally enjoys self-certainty, but this self-certainty as yet lacks truth. To be a subject, my singularity must posit itself as totality within the consciousness of the other. I must stake all my 'appearing totality', my life, against the others. I must stake it in such a way that, in the end, I can recognize myself in the other's consciousness as that particular totality that is not content to exclude the other but 'seeks the death of the other'. But, in seeking actively to encompass the death of the other, I am necessarily obliged to risk my own life. According to Hegel, it is solely by risking my own life that my freedom is tried and proved. 'The individual,' he adds, 'who has not risked his life may well be recognized as a person, but he has not attained to the truth of this recognition as an independent self-consciousness. Similarly, just as each stakes his own life, so each must seek the other's death.' (2001, p. 192 citing Hegel [1807] 1977, p. 349)

This understanding of self-consciousness, and of the violent lord–bondsman dialectic as a constitutive necessity of self-consciousness's realisation of human subjectivity and freedom, Mbembe argues, shapes Hegel's notion of self-consciousness that defines colonial cosmology and epistemology in the Introduction to the *Philosophy of History* (Mbembe 2001, p. 190). And it is also this rendition of self-consciousness that explains Mbembe's view that 'in Hegel appears the idea that affirmation of a foreign consciousness in face of mine relieves my own being of all value – and it is Hegel who pushes this idea to its extreme limits' (2001 p. 191). In this view, human self-consciousness is relieved of all its value as a human self-consciousness when it encounters a foreign human self-consciousness. In negating the humanity of the foreign self-consciousness, it takes violence for self-consciousness to regain its value as a human self-consciousness. For Mbembe, '[that] means that I am only a human being because I have made myself recognized as absolute superiority by another human being' (2001, p. 192). Hegel's denial of the humanity of sub-Saharan African subjects proves the idea that 'affirmation of a foreign consciousness in face of mine relieves my own being of all value' (2001, p. 191). Mbembe's understanding of the lord–bondsman dialectic in the *Phenomenology* becomes conscripted into the colonial reasoning seen in the *Philosophy of History*; and Hegel's lord–bondsman dialectic is presented as central to his withholding of universal historical self-consciousness from the indigenous peoples of sub-Saharan Africa. But in making this move, Mbembe presents the lord–bondsman dialectic as having been influenced and shaped by colonial events; and the distinction between the lord–bondsman shape of self-consciousness and the self-consciousness presented in the Introduction to the *Philosophy of History* is obliterated.[5] Hegel's notion of self-consciousness thus attains a single meaning across two different philosophical armatures.

Reading Hegel's different formulations of consciousness in the Introduction to the *Philosophy of History* into the lord–bondsman dialectic logically leads to the idea that the epistemological figures of the lord and the bondsman correspond to the distinction between human and animal, respectively.[6] In Mbembe's rendition, Hegel presents historical (European) self-consciousness as man-human and what I term Negro-consciousness as man-animal.[7] When these different kinds of consciousness are read into the lord–bondsman dialectic, as Mbembe does, the lord logically becomes the man-human and the bondsman becomes the man-animal. In this view, if the lord–bondsman dialectic is understood as colonial reason, it makes logical sense to construe the lord–bondsman dialectic as the relation between man-human consciousness and man-animal consciousness. But the question arises, to what extent does Mbembe's reading of Hegel's notions of self-consciousness in the *Phenomenology* and the *Philosophy of History* represent Hegel's own ideas on self-consciousness? In the sections that follow, I will show that the lord–bondsman shape of self-consciousness and the self-consciousness discussed in relation to Negro-consciousness are distinct in the two different texts.

The self-consciousness of the lord and bondsman: not all too human

In addition to being influenced by Hegel's colonial and racial discourse, Mbembe's framing of Hegel's lord–bondsman dialectic is clearly also influenced by the work of Alexandre Kojève (Mbembe 2001, p. 191). Like Fanon ([1952] 2008), as Philippe Van Haute shows in chapter two of this book, Mbembe reads Hegel's *Phenomenology* and the lord–bondsman dialectic through the lens of Kojève's reading, or at least agrees with Kojève's reading of Hegel's lord–bondsman dialectic. The translation of the lord–bondsman dialectic into the master–slave dialectic by Kojève ([1947] 1980) turns Hegel's epistemological figures into anthropological subjects. Kojève further defines history as the struggle between masters and slaves ([1947] 1980, p. 9), which is very different from Hegel's understanding of history, as I will show. And the lord–bondsman dialectic does not feature in Hegel's conception and articulation of history.[8] Mbembe's Hegel, like Fanon's Hegel, is the Kojèvian Hegel of the master–slave dialectic.

In the paragraphs on lordship and bondage and in the entire chapter on 'Self-Consciousness', Hegel does not discuss a specific defining character of self-consciousness that makes it human, as Mbembe would have it. Rather, Hegel identifies different moments and shapes of consciousness and explains how these different shapes of consciousness attain their epistemological positions and the entailed ontological conditions for the possibility of self-knowledge. To be precise, in the lord–bondsman dialectic Hegel explains how self-consciousness emerges from consciousness, progressing dialectically to the knowledge of itself as 'I am I', and the knowledge of the existence of things other than the 'I'. For my purposes here, I will give a brief epistemological account of the lord–bondsman dialectic to show that what is at stake is not whether self-consciousness is human or not, but what this particular kind of self-consciousness knows and how it comes to know what it knows.[9]

For Hegel, '[self]-consciousness is, to begin with, simple being-for-self, self-equal through the exclusion from itself of everything else. For it, its essence and absolute object is "I"' (Hegel [1807] 1977, p. 113 – §186). In its initial moment, as it emerges from consciousness, self-consciousness does not understand itself to be in relation to any object other than itself ([1807] 1977, p. 105 – §167).

The dialectic commences when 'self-consciousness is faced by another self-consciousness' ([1807] 1977, p. 111 – §179), and 'one individual is confronted by another individual' ([1807] 1977, p. 113 – §186); this is not a collective historical self-consciousness being confronted by a collective historical self-consciousness, or even a self-consciousness that has developed an understanding of the plurality of self-consciousness ('Ich, das Wir, und Wir, das Ich ist'):

Appearing thus immediately on the scene, they are for one another like ordinary objects, *independent* shapes, individuals submerged in the being [or immediacy] of Life – for the object in its immediacy is here determined as Life. They are, *for each other*, shapes of consciousness which have not yet accomplished the movement of absolute abstraction, of rooting-out all immediate being, and of being merely the purely negative being of self-identical

consciousness; in other words, they have not as yet exposed themselves to each other in the form of pure being-for-self, or as self-
consciousnesses. Each is indeed certain of its own self, but not of
the other, and therefore its own self-certainty still has no truth.
([1807] 1977, p. 113 – §186)

The individual self-consciousnesses see each other as objects to be annihilated because this shape of their self-consciousness does not have the
understanding or knowledge of difference as otherness. Hence the two
individual self-consciousnesses engage in a struggle unto death because
'in so far as it is the action of the other, each seeks the death of the other'
([1807] 1977, p. 113 – §187). 'And it is only through staking one's life
that freedom is won; only thus is it proved that for self consciousness,
its essential being is not [just] being, not the immediate form in which
it appears, not its submergence in the expanse of life, but rather that
there is nothing present in it which could not be regarded as a vanishing
moment, that it is only pure being-for-self' ([1807] 1977, p. 114 – §187).

But the actions of the individual self-consciousness must not
be taken to mean a historical self-consciousness, or people trying to
destroy each other. The two self-consciousnesses seek each other's
death because the truth of this shape of self-consciousness only allows
it to understand the other's truth as nothingness, lacking in being. The
other of this shape of self-consciousness is not the other who is a threat
to its life and security, or whose difference entails an inferior being. On
the contrary, the other of this shape of self-consciousness simply does
not appear to have being or otherness. From Hegel's point of view, the
violence that ensues from the dialectic is therefore not human violence
or dehumanising violence.[10]

By the end of the struggle or dialectic, one shape of self-consciousness
reduces itself to the position of bondsman, and the other takes the position of lord. The individual self-consciousness that reduces itself to the
condition of bondsman through work ultimately succeeds in unifying

the two *different moments* of 'I am I' and the consciousness of difference as otherness:

> But in point of fact self-consciousness is the reflection out of the being of the world of sense and perception, and is essentially the return from otherness. As self-consciousness, it is movement; but since what it distinguishes from itself is only itself as itself, the difference, as an otherness, is immediately superseded for it; the difference is not, and it [self-consciousness] is only the motionless tautology of: 'I am I'; but since for it the difference does not have the form of being, it is not self-consciousness. Hence otherness is for it in the form of a being, or as a *distinct moment*; but there is also for consciousness the unity of itself with this difference as a second distinct moment. (Hegel [1807] 1977, p. 105 – §167)

This self-consciousness emerges out of the dialectic as a shape of self-consciousness different from that which existed at the beginning of the dialectic, when it first encountered another self-consciousness. The bondsman position of self-consciousness attains its freedom from the constricting tautology of 'I am I'. It is able to see difference as otherness, and through otherness retains for itself the 'I' as an essential being amidst otherness. The self-consciousness that attains the condition of lord remains the same shape of self-consciousness as that in which it entered the dialectic, because its 'essential nature is [still] to exist only for [itself]; [it] is the sheer negative power for whom the thing is nothing' ([1807] 1977, p. 116 – §191).

Universal historical self-consciousness: all too human

In the *Philosophy of History* ([1837] 2001), Hegel traces the actual historical configurations of self-consciousness as it appears in human self-consciousness, by showing how reason, through self-consciousness, has appeared in history (and constituted history), and is dialectically progressing to absolute freedom. In describing his project in the lectures on the *Philosophy of History*, Hegel writes:

> It must be observed at the outset, that the phenomenon we investigate – Universal History – belongs to the realm of *Spirit*. The term *'World'*, includes both physical and psychical Nature. Physical Nature also plays its part in the World's History, and attention will have to be paid to the fundamental natural relations thus involved. But *Spirit*, and the course of its development, is our substantial object. Our task does not require us to contemplate Nature as a Rational System in itself – though in its own proper domain it proves itself such – but simply in its relation to *Spirit*. ([1837] 2001, p. 30)

Hegel is clearly concerned with the way in which Spirit *self-consciously* relates to itself and the rational system of nature in actual phenomena towards absolute freedom: 'the *final cause of the World at large*, we allege to be the consciousness of its own freedom on the part of Spirit, and *ipso facto*, the reality of that freedom' ([1837] 2001, p. 33). But then what is Spirit, and how does Spirit appear in World History and as World History? Allow me to quote Hegel at length:

> *Spirit*, on the contrary, may be defined as that which has its centre in itself. It has not a unity outside itself, but has already found it; it exists in and *with itself*. Matter has its essence out of itself; Spirit is *self-contained existence* (*Bei-sich-selbst-seyn*). Now this is Freedom, exactly. For if I am dependent, my being is referred to something else which I am not; I cannot exist independently of something external. I am free, on the contrary, when my existence depends upon myself. This self-contained existence of Spirit is none other than self-consciousness – consciousness of one's own being. Two things must be distinguished in consciousness; first, the fact that *I know*; secondly, *what I know*. In self-consciousness these are

merged in one; for Spirit knows itself. It involves an appreciation of its own nature, as also an energy enabling it to realize itself; to make itself *actually* that which it is *potentially*. According to this abstract definition it may be said of Universal History, that it is the exhibition of Spirit in the process of working out the knowledge of that which it is potentially. ([1837] 2001, p. 31)

Self-consciousness in the *Philosophy of History* is historical in the sense that it is tied to the movement of Spirit through World History, that is, through a 'worlded' or concrete history – quite in contrast to an ontological-epistemological understanding of the lord–bondsman dialectic of self-consciousness in the *Phenomenology*. This historical self-consciousness already has an understanding of difference as otherness and already exists in community. For Hegel, whether in 'civilised' form or 'uncivilised' form, man has always existed in social life and this is a historical fact ([1837] 2001, pp. 55–56). This is distinct from the lord–bondsman shape of self-consciousness that does not have sociality, for it enters the dialectic without an understanding of difference as otherness, which would be essential to its own historicity and the possibility for socialisation.

The shape of self-consciousness in the *Philosophy of History* is also a project of self-creation/realisation; it 'make[s] itself *actually* that which it is *potentially*' ([1837] 2001, p. 31). If this self-consciousness makes itself by realising what it is potentially, through working out the knowledge of its nature and thereby appreciating its own nature, this means that it cannot be reduced to the mere tautology of 'I am I' that we find in the lord–bondsman shape of self-consciousness. It is not even the same shape of self-consciousness as that which emerges from the lord–bondsman dialectic in the form of the bondsman. What we have here is a shape of self-consciousness that has a self-conscious relation with the natural world, its socio-historical context and itself, through reason or thought. It is through reason that this shape of self-consciousness progresses in thought and actual socio-political reality towards absolute freedom.

Emphasising the essence of reason in this historical self-consciousness, Hegel states:

> We have, on the one hand, recognized the Idea in the definite form of Freedom conscious of and willing itself – having itself alone as its object: involving at the same time, the pure and simple Idea of Reason, and likewise, that which we have called subject – self-consciousness – Spirit actually existing in the World. If, on the other hand, we consider Subjectivity, we find that subjective knowledge and will is Thought. But by the very act of thoughtful cognition and volition, I will the universal object – the substance of absolute Reason. We observe, therefore, an essential union between the objective side – the Idea – and the subjective side – the personality that conceives and wills it. ([1837] 2001, p. 64)

In this statement, Hegel argues for the necessity of a self-consciousness that sets the terms of the dialectic of universal history. This consciousness is a universal historical self-consciousness. If reason determines the terms of the dialectic of universal history, then it must be clear that it operates on conditions different from those which we find in the lord–bondsman dialectic. While the dialectic in the lord–bondsman shape of self-consciousness works to unify the two distinct moments of the tautology 'I am I' with the consciousness of difference as otherness, the dialectic in the universal historical shape of self-consciousness operates to realise the Freedom of Spirit through the freedom of men (self-consciousness) in historical societies. It allows individual subjects (States) to participate in the Universal Subject (Spirit). What is at stake in the dialectic is historical socio-political progress towards absolute freedom. In universal historical self-consciousness, the dialectic is between what Hegel defines as Necessity and Freedom: '[the] latent abstract process of Spirit being regarded as Necessity, while that which exhibits itself in the conscious will of men, as their interest, belongs to the domain of Freedom' ([1837] 2001, p. 40). Necessity as the objective

(Universal Subject and Object) and human self-consciousness as the sub-ject relate to each other dialectically in socio-political realities (the State) to attain freedom of the Universal Subject. By presenting Necessity and Freedom as the motor of universal history, Hegel's view of history stands in contrast to Kojève's view that the master–slave dialectic is the motor of history. For Hegel, the dialectic between freedom and necessity results in developed social existence that progressively gives men knowledge of their nature as free self-consciousness, and as a consequence, creates socio-political conditions that make them freer. And this development manifests itself in a better understanding and realisation of law, moral-ity and justice in a state ([1837] 2001, p. 62).

Reason is essential to this universal historical self-consciousness because 'Reason governs the world, and has consequently governed its history' ([1837] 2001, p. 40). Therefore to know the history of the world, one must know the history of Reason. This self-consciousness can participate in Universal or World History by participating in Reason: 'it must be remarked that the agents themselves [universal historical self-consciousness] are intelligent thinking beings. The purport of their desires is interwoven with general, essential considerations of justice, good, duty, etc.; for mere desire – volition in its rough and savage forms – falls not within the scene and sphere of Universal History' ([1837] 2001, p. 43). This distinction between human desire with reason directed towards justice, morality and duty on the one hand, and mere desire without reason or morality, good and duty, on the other, calls up a dif-ferent kind of self-consciousness: the Negro-consciousness. The rela-tionship between the universal historical shape of self-consciousness and Negro-consciousness is not a dialectical relationship, according to Hegel. For nowhere in the *Philosophy of History* does he argue that the universal historical self-consciousness and Negro-consciousness stand in a dialectical relation. Hegel offers slavery and cultural assimilation as educational means for Negro-consciousness to move beyond mere 'isolated sensual existence' and develop thought for participating in universal history – that is, European history ([1837] 2001, p. 117).

But Negro-consciousness should not be mistaken for the lord–bondsman shape of self-consciousness. It is a much more progressed self-consciousness, even if it may lack universal thought in Hegel's view. Unlike the lord–bondsman shape of self-consciousness, Negro-consciousness is a social self-consciousness involving an 'arbitrary sub-jective choice' and knowledge of itself and other beings around it ([1837] 2001, p. 114). It is what Mbembe describes in the following terms: 'in the African fetish, free will remains master of the image it has adopted. What Africans regard as the power of the fetish is not an objective entity with an existence distinct from that of its makers' (Mbembe 2001, p. 177). For Hegel, Negro-consciousness has not yet developed the capacity to relate to itself and others beyond mere subjective desires, in order to attain objective universality through laws, justice and morality (Hegel [1837] 2001, p. 114). From his point of view, law, morality and justice in socio-political communities are evidence of the presence of Reason and Freedom in the self-consciousness of its members. The absence of the former entails the absence of the latter, and consequently the lack of Universal History or self-conscious history (see Hegel [1837] 2001, pp. 53–57).

From the thoughts gathered so far in this discussion, it should be clear that the lord–bondsman shape of self-consciousness is dif-ferent from the Negro-consciousness and universal historical self-consciousness that Hegel discusses in the *Philosophy of History*. But then a last concern arises: what is the cost of conflating Hegel's different shapes of self-consciousness in theorisation of the processes of slavery, colonisation and liberation of sub-Saharan African subjects?

Thinking with Hegel's lord–bondsman dialectic

Mbembe's instrumentalisation of Hegel's lord–bondsman dialectic pro-duces non-agential sub-Saharan African colonial subjects. While Fanon accepts the Kojèvian notion of recognition but rejects the master–slave dialectic in the struggle for the liberation of the colonised (see Fanon [1952] 2008, pp. 45, 82–83, [1959] 1965, p. 170), Mbembe adopts the dialectic for analysing the dehumanising violence of colonialism and slavery. He writes:

> The victorious consciousness then accedes to the status of master – that is, of one who has 'proved', demonstrated, realized, and revealed his superiority over biological existence and the natural world in general. Meanwhile the defeated consciousness is reduced to the condition of *slave*. In these circumstances, the defeated's history (if indeed one can speak of history in relation to this person) can only be an animal process. But what holds for the animal holds for the colonized, as what holds for the act of colonizing holds for the act of hunting. (Mbembe 2001, p. 193)

Mbembe tells us that his Hegelian 'defeated' self-consciousness is like a colonised subject reduced to an animal process. He goes even further to argue that this defeated self-consciousness is reduced to animal processes, to the point of being hunted down like a wild animal. The colonising process, in Mbembe's view, took the form of a hunt: 'It can be understood that killing a native belongs to the same register as killing an animal or expunging something no longer of any use. But why, how, and in what circumstances does one kill an animal? From a Hegelian standpoint, what founds the act of killing an animal is simple. The animal has no respect either for itself or for others; more, nothing in it that has anything of the human' (2001, p. 193).

What Mbembe presents here as 'Hegelian' is plausible coming from the Kojèvian Hegel and the Hegel of the Introduction to the *Philosophy of History*, but not from the Hegel of the lord–bondsman dialectic. In Hegel's lord–bondsman dialectic, the self-consciousness that submits to the other (the defeated self-consciousness) is not reduced to an animal process; instead, the self-consciousness works. And through work, the bondsman self-consciousness unifies the two distinct moments of the 'I am I'. Mbembe's dialectic, on the other hand, does not consider the possibility of work in the case of the defeated self-consciousness.

Mbembe's defeated subject is drained of all that is human, and is seemingly incapable of work. But to what extent does this narrative of the process of colonisation and enslavement relate to the actual historical processes? When the analysis only captures the role of the human in opposition to the animal, the entanglement of inertias, reversals, raptures and contradictions which govern actual historical processes gets displaced (2001, pp. 13–15).

In 'African Modes of Self-Writing' (Mbembe 2002), Mbembe argues that the binary narrative of the master and slave does not permit us to consider the role that the colonised may have played in the processes of colonisation and enslavement, 'as long as continental Africans neglect to rethink slavery – not merely as a catastrophe of which they were but the victims, but as the product of a history that they ... played an active part in shaping' (2002, p. 260).[11] The master-slave narrative, in this context, produces the discourse of victimhood (2002, p. 245) which Mbembe emphatically rejects. To be sure, he is aware that modelling power relations on the master–slave dialectic can produce this discourse of victimhood: 'what might appear to be the apotheosis of voluntarism is here accompanied by a lack of philosophical depth and, paradoxically, a cult of victimization. Philosophically, the Hegelian thematics of identity and difference, as classically exemplified in the master-bondsman relationship, is surreptitiously reappropriated by the ex-colonized' (2002, p. 244). Yet he unintentionally appropriates the discourse of victimhood in modelling the dehumanising violence of slavery and colonisation on the master–slave dialectic, as in this statement in *On the Postcolony*: 'in these circumstances, the defeated's history (if indeed one can speak of history in relation to this person) can only be an animal process' (Mbembe 2001, p. 193). In this understanding of the dehumanising violence of colonialism and slavery, the history of the defeated is indeed presented as lacking in agency: 'the African is supposed to be merely a castrated subject, the passive instrument of the Other's enjoyment' (Mbembe 2002, p. 252).

The master–slave dialectic displaces the different and sometimes contradictory paths that many sub-Saharan African societies and individuals have taken (or have been forced to take) from the time of the initial presence of modern Europeans on the continent to the present. All the sub-Saharan African colonised or defeated become a people without histories, because this narrative rejects the legitimacy of local sub-Saharan thinking and histories since they have been reduced to animal processes. This de-legitimation of African thinking and histories, in turn, resonates with Hegel's view that sub-Saharan Africans lack reason and history. Consequently, in thinking with Hegel's lord–bondsman dialectic or with its master–slave interpretation as used by Mbembe, we appropriate Hegel's racist and colonial thinking from the Introduction to the *Philosophy of History* and fail to capture the actual historical processes of sub-Saharan African colonisation, slavery and liberation.

In the final analysis, while Mbembe's theorisation presents us with certain challenges concerning the historiography of enslavement and colonisation – which he explicates in other chapters of *On the Postcolony* and in his economically inflected presentation of racism in *Critique of Black Reason* (Mbembe 2017), offering insightful and nuanced accounts of racial and colonial dehumanising violence – it also raises questions about the instrumentalisation of Hegel's epistemological figures for socio-historical analysis. As intimated earlier, Mbembe's colonial reading of Hegel's lord–bondsman dialectic resonates with Kojève's reading of the dialectic. While Kojève turns Hegel's epistemological figures into Marxist sociological figures, Mbembe turns them into colonial-racist sociological figures. In both cases, we lose sight of Hegel's intended epistemological categories in the lord–bondsman dialectic.

In this chapter, I have shown that we are theoretically and historically at a loss when we, with Mbembe, conflate the different Hegelian shapes of self-consciousness, and model the violence of colonialism and enslavement on the lord–bondsman dialectic. I am not denying that the geographical basis of Hegel's *Philosophy of History* is premised on the problematic denial of the humanity of the indigenous peoples of sub-Saharan Africa. What I am arguing is that there is a difference between the shapes of self-consciousness that Hegel articulates in the lord–bondsman dialectic in the *Phenomenology*, and the shapes of self-consciousness articulated in the *Philosophy of History*. This difference does not justify construing the lord-bondman dialectic as a colonial epistemology in the way that Mbembe does; nor can it motivate modelling the socio-historical processes of colonialism and slavery on an epistemological (but non-historical, non-sociological and non-human) figuration of the lord–bondsman dialectic. The lord–bondsman dialectic does not tell us anything substantial about the actual complex historical processes of colonisation and slavery, or about their consequences which Mbembe so vividly explicates in his work.

Notes

1   By 'Africa' here I mean sub-Saharan Africa, or what Hegel considers 'Africa proper' (Hegel ([1837] 2001, p. 109); and by 'African subjects' I mean indigenous peoples of sub-Saharan Africa. I use the term 'indigenous' in this text to contrast sub-Saharan colonised and racialised peoples with European colonists of modern times. This should not imply that I deny the reality of internal African migration and historical change among indigenous peoples.

2   Neither Hegel nor Mbembe uses the term 'Negro-consciousness'. I have coined this term to capture the kind of consciousness that Hegel ascribes to his Negro subjects.

3   In addition to Merleau-Ponty, Mbembe here also references Kojève's *Introduction to the Reading of Hegel* ([1947] 1980). This would explain Mbembe's understanding of Hegel's lord–bondsman dialectic in the *Phenomenology*. This point is discussed further in the next section of the chapter.

4   The definition of self-consciousness as a 'motionless tautology', '*I am I*', that Mbembe gives here is taken from the *Phenomenology* (Hegel [1807] 1977), p. 105 – §167), on the lord–bondsman dialectic, as I will show later.

5   The attempt to read the lord–bondsman dialectic as conscripted by the events of colonialism and slavery at Hegel's time is not unique to Mbembe. Susan Buck-Morss (2000, 2009) argues that the dialectic was inspired by the Haitian Revolution (1791–1804). David Scott (2010), however, casts doubt on Buck-Morss's conjecture.

6   In the *Philosophy of History* Hegel presents this distinction in the following terms: 'The Negro, as already observed, exhibits the natural man in his

completely wild and untamed state ... there is nothing harmonious with humanity to be found in this type of character' (Hegel [1837] 2001, p. 111).

7   It is important to note that the presentation of sub-Saharan African subjects as non-human or animal-like is not Hegel's invention. Hegel was only uncritically appropriating views that were commonly held at the time, as Robert Bernasconi (1998) shows. Mbembe captures Hegel's uncritical assimilation of colonial discourse on the African subject in these words: 'Picking up rumor and gossip, amplifying them in the telling, [Hegel's position] claims to throw light on things that haunt and obsess it, but about which, in truth, it knows absolutely nothing. Thus it is endlessly chasing its own shadow' (Mbembe 2001, pp. 178–79). Hegel inflected the idea of the African subject as an animal-like subject in a novel way, giving it philosophical articulation as a particular kind of consciousness (what I have termed 'Negro-consciousness').

8   Mbembe's agreement with Kojève is evident in an endnote advocating a reading of Hegel through Kojève: 'In addition to Hegel's own assertions, quite dense and contradictory, set out primarily in *Phenomenology of Spirit*, see A. Kojève, *Introduction to the Reading of Hegel*, especially pp. 38–56' (Mbembe 2001, p. 209, n. 54).

9   In chapter two of this book, Philippe Van Haute provides a detailed exposition of the epistemological and ontological stakes entailed in Hegel's lord–bondsman dialectic.

10   Robert Bernasconi (2011) provides a close reading of Hegel's views on human violence in the *Philosophy of History*.

11   In this text, Mbembe rejects the understanding of colonialism and slavery as solely attributable to European violence. He argues that native Africans should recognise their role in these processes: 'between African Americans' memory of slavery and that of continental Africans, there is a shadowy zone that conceals a deep silence – the silence of guilt and the refusal of Africans to face up to the troubling aspect of the crime that directly engages their own responsibility. For the fate of black slaves in modernity is not solely the result of the tyrannical will and cruelty of the Other, however well established the latter's culpability may be. The other primitive signifier is the murder of brother by brother' (Mbembe 2002, p. 160).

References

Bernasconi, Robert (1998). 'Hegel at the Court of the Ashanti'. In Stuart Barnett (ed.), *Hegel after Derrida*. London: Routledge.

Bernasconi, Robert (2011). '"The ruling categories of the world": The Trinity in Hegel's *Philosophy of History* and *The Rise and Fall of Peoples'*. In Stephen Houlgate and Michael Baur (eds), *A Companion to Hegel*. Malden: Blackwell.

Buck-Morss, Susan (2000). 'Hegel and Haiti'. *Critical Inquiry* 26(4): 821–65.

Buck-Morss, Susan (2009). *Hegel, Haiti, and Universal History*. Pittsburgh: University of Pittsburgh Press.

Fanon, Frantz (1965). *A Dying Colonialism* (1959). Translated by Haakon Chevalier. New York: Grove Press.

Fanon, Frantz (2008). *Black Skin, White Masks* (1952). Translated by Charles Lam Markmann. London: Pluto Press.

Hegel, Georg Wilhelm Friedrich (1977). *Hegel's Phenomenology of Spirit* (1807). Translated by A.V. Miller. Oxford: Clarendon Press.

Hegel, Georg Wilhelm Friedrich (2001). *The Philosophy of History* (1837). Translated by John Sibree. Kitchener, Ontario: Batoche.

Kojève, Alexandre (1980). *Introduction to the Reading of Hegel: Lectures on the Phenomenology of Spirit* (1947). Assembled by Raymond Queneau, edited by Allan Bloom, translated by James H. Nichols Jr. Ithaca: Cornell University Press.

Mbembe, Achille (2001). *On the Postcolony*. Berkeley: University of California Press.

Mbembe, Achille (2002). 'African modes of self-writing'. *Public Culture* 14(1): 239–73.

Mbembe, Achille (2017). *Critique of Black Reason*. Johannesburg: Wits University Press.

Merleau-Ponty, Maurice (1962). *Phenomenology of Perception* (1945). Translated by Colin Smith. London: Routledge and Kegan Paul.

Scott, David (2010). 'Antinomies of slavery, enlightenment, and universal history'. *Small Axe* 14(3): 152–62.

5 | Struggle and Violence: Entering the Dialectic with Frantz Fanon and Simone de Beauvoir

Beata Stawarska

In this chapter I will develop an intertextual reflection on struggle and violence to rethink the dialectic of interhuman reciprocity, drawing on a broad range of Simone de Beauvoir's and Frantz Fanon's philosophical writings that share a deep intellectual commitment to the emancipation of socially subjugated groups. Several scholars have already productively interpreted Fanon's analysis of white colonial racism in *Black Skin, White Masks* (Fanon [1952] 2008) alongside Beauvoir's analysis of white patriarchy in her 1949 work *The Second Sex* (Gordon 2015; Moi 2008; Renault 2014). I propose to expand this intertextual reflection in the light of works that have received less, if any, attention amid the burgeoning Beauvoir–Fanon scholarship, namely Beauvoir's 1940s *Philosophical Writings* (Beauvoir 2012a) and Fanon's *The Wretched of the Earth* (Fanon [1961] 2004). I will argue that both thinkers expressly occupy the 'French Hegelian' dialectic of interhuman reciprocity from a subjugated personal-philosophical viewpoint, in order to envisage an emancipatory struggle for women and blacks as an urgent moral task. In doing so, I will borrow Beauvoir's analysis of violence as morally and metaphysically justified in cases of extreme human degradation, to lend moral legitimacy to Fanon's encomium to retributive violence within anticolonial resistance. Finally, I will consider the productive ambiguity of violence as bodily vitality that includes destructive/reactive expressions as well as productive enactments of novel subjective and social formations.

The encounter

An encounter between Beauvoir and Fanon did take place. They met in Rome, in July of 1961, for a three-day intellectual marathon, in the company of Jean-Paul Sartre. The meeting left an indelible mark on Beauvoir's thought; Fanon, the revolutionary intellectual, clearly stands out in her intellectual autobiography among a gallery of giants featuring Fidel Castro and Nikita Krushchev, as the figure who impressed her the most. 'He was an exceptional man,' she writes. 'When I shook his feverish hand, I seemed to be touching the very passion that was consuming him. He communicated this fire to others; when one was with him, life seemed to be a tragic adventure, often horrible but of infinite worth' (Beauvoir 1994, pp. 318–19, translation modified).

The horrors of the Algerian War (1954–62) haunt Beauvoir's intellectual autobiography (covering the years from 1952 to 1962); she pens the most uncompromising accounts of the war in Algeria, compared with those she wrote about political excesses in Cuba and the Soviet Union (Beauvoir 1994). In her descriptions of the French colonial government's widespread and tacitly approved use of torture, repeated rape and starvation of Algerian citizens, she assumes her share of responsibility as a French citizen: 'I'm French. The words scalded my throat like an admission of hideous deformity' (1994, p. 106). To be French is to pass over in complicit silence the fact that Algerian families are enduring extreme torture in the French territory (1994, p. 306). To be French is to incubate the worst imaginable disease – a loss of empathy for one's fellow human beings, a numbness in the face of deliberately inflicted, excruciating suffering (1994, p. 106). To be French is to commit what Beauvoir calls the 'absolute evil' of human degradation, whereby reciprocal recognition of dignity is replaced with what Fanon calls a Manichaean world of white colonial racism (Fanon [1961] 2004, pp. 6–7).

Beauvoir's political sentiments and activist support of the Algerian revolutionaries, for example in her defence of Djamila Boupacha, an Algerian freedom fighter (Beauvoir 1960, 2012a), and her co-signing of the open letter published as 'Manifesto of the 121' (Adamov et al. 1960), had primed her for an informed exchange with Fanon in 1961. Biographers' reports of this meeting tend to emphasise the intensity of Fanon's and Sartre's conversation (see Hayman 1987), but Beauvoir's own account suggests that she was an actively engaged participant in the meeting.[1] She reports that Fanon described the acts of violence committed against the Congolese by the Belgians and against the Angolans by the Portuguese with manifest horror – as much as when he recounted the Algerian counterviolence against the French (Beauvoir 1994, p. 316). It is as a careful reader of Fanon's text, 'De la violence' (Fanon 1961a), that Beauvoir frames his complex position on the role of violence in the colonial context, against the received view that he promoted violence at all costs.[2] And if she felt the fire that animated his feverish hand, she may have been thinking of Fanon's descriptions of the energetic body in *Black Skin, White Masks* (see for example Fanon [1952] 2008, pp. 90–93). Beauvoir read Fanon's gestures and remarks as carefully as she had read his books.

Did Fanon read Beauvoir? Did he encounter a fellow intellectual in her as he did in Sartre? Fanon's personal library included a copy of *The Second Sex* (Fanon 2015, p. 594), and he was an avid reader of *Les temps modernes*, where she had published many of her works. Beauvoir's conception of gender (Beauvoir 2011) and Fanon's conception of race (Fanon [1952] 2008) are interlinked, with the idea that one becomes and is not born woman probably prefiguring the thesis of the black as a white construction (Gordon 2015, p. 31; Renault 2014). Both adopt the French Hegelian dialectics of recognition from a subjugated point of view: of the second sex within French patriarchy, of the colonised blacks on the African continent. Even if, in their uncritical acceptance of Alexandre Kojève's reading of Hegel (Kojève [1947] 1980), they are guilty of committing a 'category mistake' and confusing the 'shapes of consciousness' represented by the lord (*Herr*) and the bondsman (*Knecht*) in Hegel's *Phenomenology of Spirit* (Hegel [1807] 1977) with the historical figures of a (white) master and a (sexual or colonial) slave (see chapters two and three by Philippe Van Haute and Ulrike Kistner in this book), they thereby mobilise the dialectic as an instrument of critique.

Beauvoir's and Fanon's Hegel (filtered through Kojève) serves to expose a gendered and racialised failure of reciprocity between men and women (Beauvoir) and between the coloniser and the colonised (Fanon), respectively. They both expressly adopt their minoritised personal-philosophical subject positions to highlight social exclusions from mutual recognition. Phenomenological description becomes wedded to social critique within both their appropriations of Hegel.

Fanon mentions Beauvoir in this context when he reports in *Black Skin, White Masks* that 'Americans staying in Paris are amazed to see the number of white women accompanied by black men. In New York, while Simone de Beauvoir was walking with Richard Wright, she was reprimanded by an old lady' (Fanon [1952] 2008, p. 160). Yet while we catch a glimpse of Beauvoir-the-white-woman-walking-in-the-company-of-a-black-man in Fanon's book, Beauvoir-the-philosopher-theorising-oppression-from-a-gendered-and-racialised-standpoint is not heard. This is troubling insofar as Fanon references the other existentialists in the notes to *Black Skin, White Masks*. Toril Moi (2008, p. 223) comments that 'Fanon's explicit invocation of Sartre and his total neglect of Beauvoir exemplify the usual response of male intellectuals to existentialism'. Lewis Gordon (2015, p. 32) observes that Beauvoir's presence at the level of ideas and her absence at the level of citation constitutes a form of 'epistemic sexism' in Fanon's work; Matthieu Renault (2014, pp. 36–37) notes a 'theoretical occultation' that is especially troubling considering the critical weight of Beauvoir's reflections on the inferiorisation of blacks in the United States, her analysis of masks and racial myths finding an echo in Fanon. Fanon's epistemic sexism and theoretical occultation of a prominent woman intellectual are a systemic reflection of their historical moment; the time is ripe to document her intellectual impact on Fanon's thought. Better yet, it is possible to read their works as generative intertexts, with potential for ongoing intellectual and political growth that enacts a shared vision of a new humanism, construed as a relational reciprocity across difference, including racial and sexual difference. An encounter, in other words.

Suffering and struggle for reciprocity

Broadly speaking, Beauvoir and Fanon adopt a dialectical model of phenomenological description whereby the subject finds itself always already imbricated in a structural situation (such as the received social norms and power relations regarding gender, race, class) *and* actively responding to and potentially revising the status quo (Stawarska 2018). While such admixtures of subjectivity and structural situation are universal to any situated human condition, Beauvoir and Fanon demonstrate that fundamental human freedom is dramatically diminished under patriarchal or colonial oppression. Women find their facticity fixed as the inessential other (Beauvoir), blacks as the dehumanised and devalued labouring bodies (Fanon). While adopting a specific subject position (of women, blacks) anchors their liberatory projects in a concrete and irreducible form of suffering, Beauvoir and Fanon both risk rendering some forms of subjectivity invisible. Beauvoir develops questions of gendered and racialised suffering as an analogy rather than a shared and intersecting condition, and thus tends to assume whiteness as a dominant if unexamined racial category (Gines 2014). Fanon does not thematise gender, and tends to theorise revolutionary subjectivity in predominantly masculinist terms (McClintock 1999). The charge of white feminism in Beauvoir and black chauvinism in Fanon needs to be taken seriously; in response, I follow Vikki Bell's suggestion in 'Owned Suffering' (Bell 2000) to focus on a shared situation of oppression that blurs essentialised identities, and to imagine forms of political connectivity that raise oppressed groups from the dominant affect of *ressentiment*. *Ressentiment* is a reactive position based on a wounded attachment to the white male bourgeois subject (Bell 2000, p. 61; Brown

1995). Bell proposes to move the political imagination beyond *ressenti-ment* to modes of relational being within and between variously sub-jugated social groups. In following her lead, I will orient the political imagination toward a focus on a shared situation of social suffering and struggle.

With that proposed orientation in mind, let me return to an inter-textual reflection on *The Second Sex* and *Black Skin, White Masks*. In both texts, the horror of social subjugation (of women, of blacks) can be deciphered as a violation of a dialectical framework of human reciproc-ity. In French metropolitan and colonial contexts, human equality and liberty operate as empty claims, preached but not practised. Beauvoir and Fanon's philosophies begin with a premise of human *in*equality, and posit emancipation (of women and blacks) as a moral and political imperative. In agreement with Hegel, Beauvoir assumes a fundamen-tal relation of hostility between consciousness and its other (Beauvoir [1949] 2011); in this view, the subject posits itself as being essential in opposition to the other, which is initially construed as the inessential object ([1949] 2011, p. 7). In principle, the other consciousness 'has an opposing reciprocal claim' and the initial claim to absoluteness is rela-tivised within the reciprocity of an intersubjective relation ([1949] 2011, p. 7). Within the patriarchal context of sexual difference, however, this relational reciprocity fails to come into effect. Here the point of view of male sovereignty asserts itself as being the essential One and subjugates the female to the status of a non-reciprocal other.

While (in a heteronormative situation) both genders experience sexual desire and (possibly) a desire for posterity, only the subordinate other internalises the need for the master into an affect (and the cor-related attitude) of hope and fear; the master does not posit his need for the (female) other ([1949] 2011, p. 9) and is therefore not made as psychically dependent on her as she is on him. Clearly, this psycho-social constellation of affects and attitudes supposes that women play an active role in weighting the dialectical process against themselves. If consciousness tends to posit itself as being the One, why do women willingly submit to the foreign view of being the other? Beauvoir the philosopher offers a slew of reasons, including the 'delights of passivity' ([1949] 2011, p. 312) and the obscure satisfaction girls and women find in their socially subordinate position ([1949] 2011, p. 10). Yet the most compelling reason for an enduring passive stance may be found in her analysis of the ways in which female bodies tend to be materialised into adopting a passive stance by prevailing social conditions during a girl's early years.

While girls and boys are both 'tomboys' at first, only girls are explicitly prohibited from resorting to physically forceful acts in the process of exploring their surroundings. As a young girl, 'she is forbidden to fight' ([1949] 2011, p. 296); 'violence in particular is not permitted to her' ([1949] 2011, p. 343). Surely brute force does not routinely play a great role in human lives, but Beauvoir observes that a spectre of potential violence haunts most masculine behaviour and provides a permanent setting for it. The idea is not that boys and men routinely have recourse to physical force (such as arm wrestling, street brawls, athletic exploits, and so on) but that it is within their reach. She writes: 'Violence is the authentic test of every person's attachment to himself, his passions, and his will; to radically reject it is to reject all objective truth, it is to isolate one's self in an abstract subjectivity; an anger or revolt that does not exert itself in muscles remains imaginary' ([1949] 2011, p. 343).

The prohibition of violence induces a separation between the mind and the muscle, the intention and its expression; this leads to an imaginary and abstracted quality of the girl's affects and attitudes that fail to translate into concerted actions. The girl loses confidence as a result. Beauvoir writes: 'To lose confidence in one's body is to lose confidence in one's self. One needs only to see the importance that young men give to their muscles to understand that every subject grasps his body as his objective expression' ([1949] 2011, p. 344).

The real obstacle for women is that they do not learn the lesson of violence ([1949] 2011, p. 345), and that their affects do not find direct expression in their actions. If they did, girls would be less likely to assume the inferior status imposed upon them at an early age, and their subjectivity would be less likely to be overdetermined by psychic servitude. As it is, girls and women are locked into the position of *ressentiment*. Unlike the other socially subordinated groups, they do not actively struggle for liberation.

Like Beauvoir's study of white patriarchy, Fanon's analysis of colonial racism deploys a dialectically expanded view of subject and structure. Colonisation intersects with the objective historical conditions and with the human attitude toward these conditions (Fanon [1952] 2008, p. 67). The objective white minority does not feel inferiorised by the majority of the population in apartheid South Africa ([1952] 2008, p. 68) or Martinique ([1952] 2008, p. 73). The racist minority inferiorises the subject of colour ([1952] 2008, p. 73), and retroactively engenders the psychic complex of so-called inferiority, better described as a feeling of non-existence, to underscore its *socio*genesis ([1952] 2008, p. 118). Just like the feelings of fear and passivity noted by Beauvoir in women, this feeling is real in a colonised subject and it has paralysing effects ([1952] 2008, p. 118). The externally imposed paralysis is internalised as an action-bearing attitude and affect; it is an enforced pathological state that Fanon likens to the humility experienced by an amputee or an invalid ([1952] 2008, p. 119). The colonising process disciplines the colonised body into a docile, diminished and devitalised thing. Yet in the Fanonian ontology, the body remains in equal parts an effect of sociogenesis and a site of revolt: 'I refuse this amputation. I am a soul as vast as the world, a soul as deep as the deepest of rivers; my chest has the power to expand to infinity' ([1952] 2008, p. 119).

In Fanon's reading of French Hegelian dialectics, the claim to interpersonal reciprocity assumes a form of struggle from the start. Fanon notes that the white colonial master 'laughs at' ('*se moque de*') the consciousness of the slave; he does not seek recognition but only the labour of the slave ([1952] 2008, p. 195 n. 1). As Van Haute explains (in chapter two of this book), mutual recognition supposes that both parties are part of the same genus and belong to the same history; if this prior condition of 'primordial inclusion' is not met, the dialectic will not get off the ground. Accordingly, the issue for the black slave theorised by Fanon is not an absence of recognition at a historical moment but a forced exit from the movement of history. The black slave will need to assume subjectivity by his own means if he is to enter the dialectic. He will need to ascend from the level of labouring bodies to the world of moral dignity. That is why direct abolitionist struggle is preferable to having the master proclaim the end of slavery. The struggle of life and death generates new values and revitalises the body, and it makes a palpable difference to the one who will have staked his old life, risked and conquered death, and emerged as a free subject at the other end. The fight carries him to 'actional' being ([1952] 2008, p. 197) whereby he acquires a taste of action that exceeds a simple reaction filled with resentment.

In situating the dialectical process in a non-idealised site of combat, Fanon helps to thematise it in more concrete and transformative terms. Here affects, attitudes and actions form an interdependent and evolving complex; the affect and attitude of powerlessness restrain action, but a risked, unauthorised action leaves a psychic imprint of a newly found authority that may in turn translate into more (self-authorised) action. While the Fanonian affect internalises externally imposed actions within the process of enforced inferiorisation, it is also retroactively transformed by self-generated actions and their psychic aftermath. The psychic and the political are intermeshed, in that the political struggle reworks psychic dispositions and effects an inner metamorphosis. Fanon reverses the idealist understanding of action as following upon an intention; within a retroactive constitution of an actional I, intentions emerge *post actum*; the verb is not a predicate appended to a pre-existing subject but its productive source. 'Struggle, therefore I am' may be a close rendering of subject formation in Fanon. The retroactive constitution of the actional I points a way out of the passive stance. Women will *feel* more ready for struggle the more they actively engage in it; they will feel less powerless the more they practise the power they didn't know they had. Fanon's analysis of an emerging revolutionary self provides insight into how women may learn the lesson of violence *otherwise*, and be psychically transformed by a leap into action.

The moral legitimacy of violence (for Beauvoir)

I will now narrow the focus of the discussion from liberation struggle, construed as a broad French Hegelian theme, to the more morally charged question of how resorting to violence may be legitimated in the context of such a struggle. In her early, lesser-known philosophical writings (in the essay 'An Eye for an Eye', in particular [Beauvoir (1946) 2012b]), Beauvoir thematises violence as a metaphysically and morally imperative response to extreme human degradation. Her overt task in this piece is to provide a rationale for refusing to sign a petition urging the pardon of Robert Brasillach, the editor of a fascist newspaper, *Je suis partout* (1935–43), who published a column revealing the pseudonyms and whereabouts of French Jews who could eventually be deported to concentration camps. The plea for his pardon circulated by other French intellectuals was refused, and Brasillach was executed by firing squad in February 1945. Beauvoir's rationale for why Brasillach deserved to die provides an opportunity for her to develop a philosophical reflection on the moral significance of human reciprocity, and on the imperative to restore it, by means including vengeful violence, in cases where such reciprocity has been violated.

From a moral standpoint, death, suffering and captivity are not abominable in themselves. For Beauvoir, '[an] abomination arises only at the moment that a man treats fellow men like objects, when by torture, humiliation, servitude, assassination, one denies them their existence as men' (Beauvoir [1946] 2012b, p. 248). Such degradation of a human being into a thing constitutes 'the absolute evil' that calls for vengeance ([1946] 2012b, p. 248). Absolute evil exposes the false objectivity of a Kantian ethics that subsumes any particular case under a universal law ([1946] 2012b, p. 258). Here 'the accused exists in his singularity, and his concrete presence does not take on the guise of an abstract symbol so easily' ([1946] 2012b, p. 258). Punishment is not founded on rational deliberation; it is founded on hatred, a principle of prompt and passionate justice ([1946] 2012b, p. 258). In this instance, 'vengeance strives to re-establish a reciprocity of interhuman relations' that Beauvoir posits as 'the metaphysical basis of the idea of justice' ([1946] 2012b, p. 249). To avenge torture or servitude – as in the case of the concentration camp inmates who executed their Nazi jailers at the hour of liberation – is to restore the balance of human reciprocity whereby victims rise to the status of human subjects in the face of former oppressors. They settle the accounts by means of the sole effective strategy: a cathartic repetition of subjugation in reverse, a replay of tyranny from a previously excluded, mortified standpoint. Vengeful reciprocity restores the humanity of former victims by means of a quid pro quo retribution; reconciliation may come later, if at all.

Vengeful reciprocity marks an exit from the prior condition of moral and metaphysical mortification. Importantly, the vengeful act has no goal additional to this cathartic recovery of dignity. Its telos is confined to the act itself, and it serves to elevate those who were thrown into the zone of non-being back to humanity. Its metaphysical force is found in this return to the zone of being, a recovery of an almost conquered subjectivity by conquering the oppressor's consciousness, breaking his will. Its moral force is found in the restoration of the basic human value without which no liveable society is possible: a community of subjects who experience their facticity in an ambiguous manner, one that forestalls the moment of the absolute evil of utter degradation. Resorting to violence is justified in this context; it is a sacrificial, cleansing violence that can heal the wound of moral and metaphysical degradation. To turn the other cheek would be to remain wretched for life; one must avenge to re-enter the world of shared human dignity.

Despite the arguments Beauvoir presents in its defence in this work, 'An Eye for An Eye' does not glorify vengeful violence, nor does she believe its success is ever free from risk. She concedes that 'all punishment is partially a failure' ([1946] 2012b, p. 259), and that there is no exact match between crime and retribution. Punishment is rarely as prompt and as passionate as that carried out by former concentration camp inmates on their SS jailers at the hour of liberation. More often than not, the acts of tyranny and penalty are removed from each other in space and time, and one can no more avenge the dead than one can resurrect them ([1946] 2012b, pp. 251–52). There is a risk of revenge being driven by will to power rather than will to reciprocity, and a risk of revenge transforming itself into tyranny that adds another abomination to the face of the earth. False accusations may be directed at innocent parties, as was the case after the liberation of France in 1945. In all cases, a fair trial is necessary, and one must follow the legal process with all its pomp and ceremony. Beauvoir does not advocate forgoing due process when confronting a Nazi collaborator like Brasillach. Instead, she recovers the perspectives of the survivors who justifiably feel hate-filled rage toward the evildoer, and who are in the right to seek vengeance. In expressly adopting the perspective of the survivor rather than the impersonal viewpoint of Kantian ethics, she exposes the personal behind the public figure of the law, the singular at odds with the presumed objectivity of human universals.

In sum, Beauvoir's philosophical reflections on violence stress its socially pervasive quality and make a case for its moral and metaphysical legitimacy in cases of human degradation. She assumes the violent basis of all human action, but she avoids a tone of moral certitude when condoning retributive violence against unspeakable crimes. She thus steers clear of the twin risks that Judith Butler identifies in most discourses on violence versus non-violence (Butler 2009, pp. 172–77): the disavowal and the moralisation of violence. Disavowal of violence is an attitude of a beautiful soul that seeks an ethics of purity, grounded in moral certitude that imagines simple, ideal virtues; here violence is unequivocally condemned as bad, and the (presumed) violence-exempt virtues are praised as being good. Moralisation of violence similarly rests on moral certitude, but it turns violence into a virtue; a righteous glorification of impulsive hatred, it makes a move to retribution quickly and without afterthought. Disavowal and moralisation both rest on a polarised ethics of good and evil, but they assign good and evil differently. Non-violence is a pure good for the one, violence an impure but equally virtuous good for the other. Both views are wedded to a moral absolutism that cannot tolerate moral ambiguity and hesitation. Beauvoir forestalls the moment of an easy decision, and adopts an attitude of moral uncertainty in her reflections on violence. She acknowledges the intrinsically ambiguous character of moral action, and the perennial potential for excess and abuse. While she condones violence as a reparative measure against absolute evil, she does not idealise it as an absolute good. Violence may manifest itself in socially disastrous ways, but it demands that we find non-mortifying ways of inhabiting it. We become morally responsible when we thoughtfully assume the role violence plays within our moral life, and develop principles and practices, fully fallible (as Butler reminds us), that express rageful demands. These principles and practices do not act in obedience to a formal law; instead they 'craft aggression into modes of expression' (Butler 2009, p. 177), with all the risks and failures that the process entails. I propose to adopt this morally hesitant approach as a heuristic framework for an examination of Fanon's politics in the concluding section of this chapter. Following Beauvoir's lead, I hope to show that Fanon's reflections on violence should be situated at the level of moral action, and that violence as he invokes it is morally ambiguous, in that it is a negative, annihilating, as well as life-affirming principle and practice.

The politics of violence (for Fanon)

In *The Wretched of the Earth*, Fanon conceptualises violence in three distinct albeit interconnected ways (Fanon [1961] 2004). First, there is the 'objective' violence implicated in the mechanisms of domination carried out by the French colonial state. This violence is disavowed insofar as the state professes a universal humanism, but operates on the back of mass-scale white colonial racism. The state imposes a morally perverse order wherein crimes against humanity are perpetuated under a banner of equality, fraternity and liberty. While these presumably universal values should in principle encompass the coloniser and the colonised, colonial practice excludes the colonised from the human realm and perpetuates dehumanising violence behind the façade of a 'civilizing mission'. Yet the colonised do not figure solely as the victimised other for the racist subject; they also supply a demystifying epistemic perspective on the presumed universal values as tools of subjugation, whose efficacy is contingent on being stated with violence, impregnated with aggressiveness ([1961] 2004, p. 8). The colonised know what the coloniser disavows: the 'civilizing mission' preaches but does not practise human equality. The massacres of the Algerian people 'count for nothing', whereas the deaths of Frenchmen are individually reported and give rise to the greatest indignation ([1961] 2004, p. 47). The presumed universal values of liberty, fraternity and equality are exposed as white values that mask a de facto state of enslavement, alienation and inequality.

According to Fanon, the colonised are therefore justified in embracing the violence the coloniser disavows, and adopting it as a moral measure that can restore human values ([1961] 2004, p. 9). The colonised demystify the im/moral order that deploys violence to conquer and divide the Algerian people, and install a new 'ethical universe', a morality of struggle ('morale de la lutte') emerging out of the struggle for existence (Renault 2011, p. 159). In the Algerian Revolution, the instinct for self-preservation mutates into a value and a truth (Fanon [1959] 2001, p. 177; Renault 2011, p. 161). What could be theorised away as a simple biological instinct is transformed in the morality of struggle into an aspirational humanism whose goal is not only to be recognised as a human but to make oneself into one (Renault 2011, p. 161). In this moral project, violence is recovered initially as part of organised insurgency, and then as a unifying force for the colonised and a cleansing force for the individual. We find here the other two strands of violence Fanon identifies in the context of anticolonial struggle: a negative, reactive anticolonial measure; and an intrinsic force of the colonised social and individual body as it gathers moral and physical strength. The former consists of a dialectical inversion of colonial violence, an eye-for-an-eye vengefulness that can – if Fanon's argument holds in principle and in practice – morph into a life-affirming force transcending wounded attachments to the oppressor, to enact novel subjective and social formations. Violence is a liberatory praxis that initially turns accumulated terror against the coloniser, and eventually catalyses spiritual renewal, a renewed sense of dignity, and collective unity for the colonised (Balibar 2009, p. 122).

According to Fanon, vengeful violence provides the sole adequate response to the violence of the colonial regime (Fanon [1961] 2004, p. 46). Since reciprocity cannot be meaningfully restored at the levels of the courts of justice (the Algerians cannot reasonably hope that the colonial courts will make restitution for the damage caused by the colonial regime), the only moral response is to lift Algerians out of their wretched condition through the liberation struggle. It is the collapse of ordinary morality that justifies recourse to the extraordinary measure of extra-judicial violence. Just as the absolute evil of human degradation signalled a collapse of the Kantian viewpoint of universal rationality in Beauvoir's 'An Eye for an Eye', the Manichaean order of colonial racism marks an exit from the ordinary morality of shared human values in Fanon's *Wretched of the Earth*. Rather than seeking to expand the presumably universal but de facto white values to include the colonised, the colonised act on the level of the singular struggle that can assure their survival as a people, mobilising the concrete reality of their suffering *and* resisting bodies as drivers of social and moral change.

The colonised wilfully assume the violence that the coloniser disavows. Fanon writes: 'On the logical plane, the Manichaeism of the colonist produces a Manichaeism of the colonized. The theory of the "absolute evil of the colonist" is a response to the theory of the "absolute evil of the native"' ([1961] 2004), p. 50). Here we find a 'term-for-term correspondence between the two arguments' ([1961] 2004), p. 50): the violent dehumanisation of the colonised is reflected in the vengeful violence against the coloniser. While this may sound like a blind, reflexive response, Fanon's encomium on anticolonial violence is morally legitimate. Recall Beauvoir's insistence on the moral significance of human reciprocity, and on the imperative to restore it if it has been violated. Human reciprocity has a moral dimension of what ought to be and what is not, for the oppressed; hence the imperative to retain or recover a social world where others are treated – and if need be, forcefully assert themselves – as free subjects. In cases of blatant violation of this moral principle, such as colonial racism, violent action by the oppressed avenges colonial servitude, and it elevates the victims to the status of human subjects. Vengeful violence annuls the mortification engendered by the Manichaean order; it installs a moral and metaphysical arrangement where the subjugated recover their subjectivity. Crucially, Fanon's call to violence has the force of a moral imperative when situated in the framework provided by Beauvoir. In this framework, retribution works in the service of reciprocity even if it does not immediately entail reconciliation between the colonised and the coloniser; the moral force of retribution rests with the colonised and it operates primarily for their sake. For Beauvoir and Fanon, vengeful retribution is morally legitimate, whether or not it leads to a reconciliatory repair of former degrading relations between the coloniser and the colonised. Vengeful retribution is a necessary condition of reestablishing the subjectivity of the colonised, a condition *sine qua non* of entering a dialectic of reciprocity with their former oppressors.

As a subject-engendering process, anticolonial violence morphs into the third strand of a dignifying and spiritually renewing process. This strand is inscribed with positive, transformative features: it unifies the people through a common cause of nation-building, whereas colonial violence fractures and divides the nation into warring tribes ([1961] 2004, p. 51). On an individual level, violence acts as a 'cleansing force': 'It rids the colonized of their inferiority complex, of their passive and despairing attitude. It emboldens them, and restores their self-confidence ... Violence hoists the people up to the level of the leader'

([1961] 2004, p. 51). 'Enlightened by violence', the people develop a 'ravenous taste for the tangible' ([1961] 2004, p. 52). Violence emerges in its third strand as a non-reactive, socially and individually constructive force. On the social level, violence becomes a vehicle of unity, a people-power that animates, energises and illuminates an emerging communal consciousness. On the individual level, it cleanses the past condition of utter degradation and elevates the individual body to the status of a moral subject.

Importantly, violence is construed by Fanon very broadly, as bodily vitality. As Jean Bergeret recalls (Bergeret 2014, p. 9), the term 'violence' is derived from the Indo-European radicals indicating the idea of 'the vital/vitality': 'La violence, en quelque sorte, c'est la vie' ('In a way, violence is life itself'). Renault explains that 'it is first of all a natural violence, emerging from the life instinct construed as an instinct of survival, legitimate defense' (Renault 2011, p. 141). Fanon's plea for violence is, then, a plea to restore the life of the colonised (by taking it away from the coloniser who endangers it). His vitalism provides the basis for the right to self-defence; it legitimates self-defence insofar as it posits life as a value to be defended rather than as a bare fact of nature. Fanon's vitalism consists in the recovery, cultivation and transmutation of 'natural' violence into a form of ethically responsible and socially sustainable vitality. Vitalism so construed crosses the border between the natural/biological and the ethical/social domains, in that it appropriates the already present attachment to life and crafts it into principles and practices of a good (or a better) life, a life that is worth living.

That is why, for Fanon, the violence of the colonised is a profoundly bodily response as well as an act of political resistance. It operates at a deep muscular level as hypertension, as accumulated and sedimented aggressivity. Fanon notes the frequency of muscular dreams where '[the] colonized man ... is forever dreaming of becoming the persecutor' (Fanon [1961] 2004, p. 16); he is perpetually irritated by the symbols of colonial dominance that 'serve as inhibitors as well as stimulants to fight', as 'obstacles [that] actually escalate action' ([1961] 2004, p. 17).

The result is a 'pseudo-petrification', accompanied by increased muscular tension that can erupt into bloody infighting between groups and individuals ([1961] 2004, p. 17). Fratricidal struggles are one way of expressing the bottled-up violence; the other is a muscular orgy where 'the most brutal aggressiveness and impulsive violence are channelled, transformed, and spirited away' ([1961] 2004, p. 19). For example, a 'permissive dance circle' enables a cathartic explosion of erotic and aggressive energy that gives way to serenity and stillness ([1961] 2004, p. 20). The political challenge will be to capitalise on the stock of bodily energy in the struggle for liberation, 'to seize this violence as it realigns itself' ([1961] 2004, p. 21).

Fanon's account has been construed as a 'purely' biological response that operates at a level beyond moral reflection and political action. Hannah Arendt famously wondered if it is not dangerous to resort to 'organic metaphors', considering that colonial and racial issues have already been overdetermined by biological arguments (Arendt 1970; Renault 2011, p. 149). Arendt considers Fanon's 'biological justification of violence' to be dangerous (Arendt 1970; Renault, 2011, p. 155). While for Fanon (and Sartre), in violence 'is man reconstructing himself' (Sartre [1961] 2004, p. lv), for Arendt an animalic/biological struggle cannot become transformed into a political one (Renault 2011, p. 155). It must be noted, however, that for Fanon the muscular tension indicates a degree of resistance to colonial oppression, a preparation for action, and thus an opening to a better life to come. The muscular self passes a moral judgement on the colonial hierarchy as being unjust and needing to be displaced; that is why the symbols of colonial dominance intended to intimidate are registered as stimulants to action that plays out in the dream realm, orgiastic dance, fratricidal struggle and eventually guerrilla fighting. Similarly, the so-called indolence or apathy of the colonised in a forced labour context is a 'conscious way of sabotaging the colonial machine; on the biological level it is a remarkable system of self-preservation and, if nothing else, a positive curb on the occupier's stranglehold over the entire country' (Fanon [1961] 2004, p. 220).

The non-cooperation with the coloniser, the need to 'have the slightest effort literally dragged out of him' ([1961] 2004, p. 220), is an active strategy of resistance wherein bodily inertia counteracts the colonising effort and protects the colonised life. And when tortured, one can at least 'reestablish [one's] weight as a human being' by 'weigh[ing] as heavily on your torturer's body so that his wits ... can at last be restored to their human dimension' ([1961] 2004, p. 221).

Fanon's 'organic metaphors' are therefore morally coded as principled practices of retaining, restoring, reclaiming, affirming life (even in the agony of torture). Here vitality is ambiguously situated between the realms of an already given biological life and a life that shelters life. The moral subject has 'descended' to the muscular level, or better said, the moral subject is revealed as a muscular one from the start. Just as the Manichaean order operates simultaneously at an im/moral level of devaluing the colonised and degrading the body (via famine, torture, rape, crowded quarters), the order of the struggle involves a creation of new moral values and a corporeal transformation of the people from violable objects to violent subjects whose bodies are weapons, or at least heavy weights. On this reading, Fanon's violence is construed broadly as bodily vitality in the double sense of an ontologically pre-given life and a morally striving life that actively shelters life. Violence of this kind is therefore a life-affirming principle and practice wherein violence is 'owned' as an enabling, sustaining, as well as implosive bodily energy. Despite her disagreement with Fanon regarding this fundamental violence, Butler's recent work on the ontology of the body and its normative implications comes curiously close to his project (Butler 2009). For Butler it is vulnerability – not violence – that links embodiment and ethics, in that vulnerability calls into question the ontology of individualism, bringing human connectedness to the fore. Vulnerability implies (even though it does not entail) certain normative consequences (Butler 2009, p. 32). Here the ontology of the body serves as a starting point for rethinking ethical responsibility (2009, p. 32), including a responsibility for bodies lost in war, and their right to be grieved.

Drawing on Fanon, I propose an ontology of a violent body that similarly implies certain normative consequences. Butler suggests that ethical responsibility '"owns" aggression' and 'crafts [it] into modes of expression that protect those one loves' (2009, p. 177); this responsibility 'gives rise to a certain ethical practice, itself experimental, that seeks to preserve life better than it destroys it' (2009, p. 177). She concludes that this practice 'is not a principle of non-violence' (2009, p. 177); rephrased as a positive claim, ethical responsibility may in some cases be a principle of violence. Butler does not go that far, but she concedes that even the possibility of non-violence emerges because one is mired in violence, and that a thick and fitful struggle is entailed in the process (2009, p. 171). For her, '[the] struggle against violence accepts that violence is one's own possibility', and supposes a subject who 'is injured, rageful, disposed to violent retribution' (2009, p. 171). The possibility of violence is therefore implicated within an ethics of socially responsible living. Yet Butler's emphasis on vulnerability or precariousness rests on a presumption of victimisation, where one is violable or injurable but not violent (2009, p. 179). Fanon's ontology of the body suggests that one is violable as well as violent. Importantly, actively assuming violence does not entail inviolability. Fanon's studies of colonial war and mental disorders in the concluding chapter of *The Wretched of the Earth*, 'Colonial War and Mental Disorders' (Fanon [1961] 2004, pp. 181–234), provide a disconcerting testimony of inherently injurable minds and bodies.[3] Yet starting with his ontology of the body, aggression can be better owned and crafted into ethically responsible modes of living. This ontology avoids the risk of disavowing violence from a position of moral superiority, and of turning the aggression against oneself in a form of moral sadism that passes off persecution as a virtue.

Towards martial morality

My reading of Beauvoir and Fanon therefore differs from those who condemn violence insofar as it is said to result unavoidably in an unending chain of retributions (Renault 2011, p. 172) and to reproduce the deadly function of colonial racism (Mbembe 2016, p. 172). These readings do not take account of the productive moral ambiguity of violence as a negative and a positive force, an ontological given and an ethical task; they tend to disavow the violent base of political movements. To affirm life with Fanon is to acknowledge the destructive and affirmative work of violence, its energetically cataclysmic and curative capacity. On this reading, Fanon can be recruited as an 'imperfect profeminist' (Roberts 2004, p. 153). As Nada Elia observes in 'Violent Women: Surging into Forbidden Quarters' (Elia 2000), a complete reversal of the Manichaean order entails reversing and ultimately dissolving the binary opposition between the coloniser and the colonised *as well as* between a virile masculine subject and a violable female body. Nothing prevents women of colour from, in the words of Elia's title, 'surging into forbidden quarters' traditionally associated with masculinity like military combat and law enforcement. A 'good' or a morally mixed violence effectively blurs gender lines in that it foregrounds the human body as an energetic field of cultivable and communicable forces. Violence, broadly construed, supports a martial morality based on the right of socially subjugated groups to self-defence (Dorlin 2017). Martial morality relies upon an intrinsic ambiguity of violence, its destructive and productive force. It puts forward a principled practice of moral and physical regeneration that blurs essentialised identities, and directs focus to multiple forms of political connectivity within and between variously subjugated social groups. The political imagination can then be steered away from moral purism, self-directed persecution and wounded attachments of *ressentiment* toward moral ambiguity, cultivation of life-affirming practices and a multiplicity of political affects.

Notes

1   Sartre is reported to have interrupted his usual writing schedule to listen to Fanon; the one mention of Beauvoir has her 'plead[ing] that Sartre needed sleep' (Hayman 1987, pp. 384–85). Similarly, according to the chronological notes in *Écrits sur l'alienation et la liberté*, Beauvoir picked Fanon up at the airport, but only Sartre is mentioned as Fanon's interlocutor during the three-day meeting (Fanon 2015, p. 660).

2   This text was first published in *Les temps modernes* in May 1961(Fanon 1961a), and included in *Les damnés de la terre* published in October 1961 (Fanon 1961b).

3   See Nigel Gibson and Roberto Beneduce's *Frantz Fanon, Psychiatry and Politics* (2017) for a discussion of the psychic aftermath of the colonial and anticolonial violence, indicating a tension between Fanon's position as a political revolutionary and as a psychiatrist working with traumatised survivors of the Algerian War. On their reading, Fanon's view of violence needs to reflect his political as well as his psychiatric commitments.

References

Adamov, Arthur, Mandouze, André, Antelme, Robert, et al. (1960). 'Manifesto of the 121: Declaration on the right of insubordination in the Algerian War'. *Vérité-Liberté* 6 September, n.p.

Arendt, Hannah (1970). *On Violence*. Orlando: Houghton Mifflin Harcourt.

Balibar, Étienne (2009). 'Reflections on *Gewalt*'. *Historical Materialism* 17(1): 99–125.

Beauvoir, Simone de (1960). 'Pour Djamila Boupacha'. *Le Monde*, 3 June, n.p.

Beauvoir, Simone de (1994). *Hard Times: Force of Circumstance (The Autobiography of Simone de Beauvoir)*, vol. 2. Translated by Richard Howard. New York: Paragon House.

Beauvoir, Simone de (2011). *The Second Sex* (1949). Translated by Constance Borde and Sheila Malovany-Chevallier. New York: Vintage Books.

Beauvoir, Simone de (2012a). *Philosophical Writings*. Edited by Margaret A. Simons, Marybeth Timmermann and Mary Beth Mader. Urbana and Chicago: University of Illinois Press.

Beauvoir, Simone de (2012b). 'An eye for an eye' (1946). In Margaret A. Simons, Marybeth Timmermann and Mary Beth Mader (eds), *Philosophical Writings*. Urbana and Chicago: University of Illinois Press.

Bell, Vikki (2000). 'Owned suffering'. In Sara Ahmed, Jane Kilby, Celia Lury, Maureen McNeil and Beverley Skeggs (eds), *Transformations: Thinking Through Feminism*. New York: Routledge.

Bergeret, Jean (2014). *La violence fondamentale*. Paris: Dunod.

Brown, Wendy (1995). *States of Injury*. Princeton: Princeton University Press.

Butler, Judith (2009). *Frames of War: When is Life Grievable?* New York: Verso.

Dorlin, Elsa (2017). *Se défendre: Philosophie de la violence*. Paris: Éditions La Découverte.

Elia, Nada (2000). 'Violent women: Surging into forbidden quarters'. In Lewis Gordon, T. Denean Sharpley-Whiting and Renee T. White (eds), *Fanon: A Critical Reader*. Malden, MA: Blackwell.

Fanon, Frantz (1961a). 'De la violence'. *Les temps modernes* 181 : 1453–93.

Fanon, Frantz (1961b). *Les damnés de la terre*. Paris: Éditions Maspéro.

Fanon, Frantz (2001). *L'an V de la révolution Algérienne* (1959). Paris: Éditions La Découverte.

Fanon, Frantz (2004). *The Wretched of the Earth* (1961). Translated by Richard Philcox. New York: Grove Press.

Fanon, Frantz (2008). *Black Skin, White Masks* (1952). Translated by Richard Philcox. New York: Grove Press.

Fanon, Frantz (2015). *Écrits sur l'aliénation et la liberté*, vol. 1. Paris: Éditions La Découverte.

Gibson, Nigel C. and Beneduce, Roberto (2017). *Frantz Fanon, Psychiatry and Politics*. Johannesburg: Wits University Press.

Gines, Kathryn T. (2014). 'Comparative and competing frameworks of oppression in Simone de Beauvoir's *The Second Sex*'. *Graduate Faculty Philosophy Journal* 35(1–2): 251–73.

Gordon, Lewis R. (2015). *What Fanon Said: A Philosophical Introduction to His Life and Thought*. New York: Fordham University Press.

Hayman, Ronald (1987). *Sartre: A Life*. New York: Simon and Schuster.

Hegel, Georg Wilhelm Friedrich (1977). *Hegel's Phenomenology of Spirit* (1807). Translated by A.V. Miller. Oxford: Oxford University Press.

Kojève, Alexandre (1980). *Introduction to the Reading of Hegel: Lectures on the Phenomenology of Spirit* (1947). Assembled by Raymond Queneau, edited by Allan Bloom, translated by James H. Nichols Jr. Ithaca: Cornell University Press.

Mbembe, Achille (2016). *Politiques de l'inimitié*. Paris: Éditions La Découverte.

McClintock, Anne (1999). 'Fanon and gender agency'. In Nigel Gibson (ed.), *Rethinking Fanon: The Continuing Dialogue*. Amherst: Humanity Books.

Moi, Toril (2008). *Simone de Beauvoir: The Making of an Intelligent Woman*. New York: Oxford University Press.

Renault, Matthieu (2011). *Frantz Fanon: De l'anticolonialisme à la critique postcoloniale*. Paris: Éditions Amsterdam.

Renault, Matthieu (2014). 'Le genre de la race: Fanon, lecteur de Beauvoir'. *Actuel Marx* 55(1): 36–48.

Roberts, Neil (2004). 'Fanon, Sartre, violence, and freedom'. *Sartre Studies International* 10(2): 139–60.

Sartre, Jean-Paul (2004). 'Preface' (1961). In Frantz Fanon, *The Wretched of the Earth*. Translated by Richard Philcox. New York: Grove Press.

Stawarska, Beata (2018). 'Subject and structure in feminist phenomenology: Re-reading Beauvoir with Butler'. In Sara Cohen Shabot and Christinia Landry (eds), *Rethinking Feminist Phenomenology: Theoretical and Applied Perspectives*. Lanham, MD: Rowman and Littlefield.

6 | Shards of Hegel: Jean-Paul Sartre's and Homi K. Bhabha's Readings of *The Wretched of the Earth*

Reingard Nethersole

'Oh Frantz, the wretched of the earth again.' The legacy of Fanon leaves us with questions; his virtual, verbal presence among us only provokes more questions.

— Homi K. Bhabha, 'Foreword: Framing Fanon', p. x

In his 2003 address to the Council for the Development of Social Science Research in Africa (Codesria), 'Fanon and the Possibility of Postcolonial Critical Imagination', Ato Sekyi-Otu draws attention to the 'demonstrable differences in situations of reading, alternative hermeneutic circumstances, always the province of finite histories and particular spaces of political existence'. No 'situations of reading' better illuminate such historically and geographically situated differences than Jean-Paul Sartre's ([1961] 2004b) and Homi K. Bhabha's (2004) readings of Frantz Fanon's iconic text, *The Wretched of the Earth* (Fanon [1961] 2004). Both penned prefatory texts to it, Sartre a Preface to the original French edition, *Les Damnés de la Terre* (Sartre 1961), and Bhabha a Foreword to the English edition of 2004 (Bhabha 2004). Shards of Georg Wilhelm Friedrich Hegel's *Phenomenology of Spirit* (Hegel [1807] 1977) perforate both paratexts;[1] they are plain to see in Sartre's Hegel-inflected encounters, but difficult to spot in Bhabha's text with its avoidance of such inflections. Sartre reads Fanon in an international Cold War setting, anxiously grappling with the politics of decolonisation in Africa and East Asia in the late 1950s. Bhabha (re)reads Sartre *and* Fanon from a very different time and place, defined by the economic globalisation of the new millennium. Sartre's dramatically combative tone forces the reader to recognise in Fanon's call for Algeria's liberation, uttered on the brink of independence, the moment in which the 'Third World discovers *itself* and speaks to *itself* through this voice' (Sartre [1961] 2004b, p. xlvi). More than a generation later, Bhabha, citing an interview with Stuart Hall (Bhabha 2004, p. viii) reappraises with hindsight what had become, in Hall's words, the 'Bible of decolonisation'; he considers *The Wretched of the Earth* to be a handbook that still speaks to the 'dispossessed' (2004, p. xl). In his Foreword, 'Framing Fanon', and leaning heavily on David Macey's magisterial biography (Macey 2001), he presents Fanon's life and legacy as driven by 'the fraught and fervent desire for freedom' (Bhabha 2004, p. xli). But this 'legacy', together with 'his virtual, verbal presence among us', Bhabha contends, 'only provokes more questions' (2004, p. x). To a significant extent, these questions are driven by persistent master–slave ascriptions derived from Alexandre Kojève's 1930s Hegel lectures (Kojève [1947] 1980) that are still coursing through the literature on postcolonialism and decolonisation.

Readers usually skip forewords, despite their function as pathways to a text's thematics. They also tend to overlook the fact that such introductory paratexts often provide telling insights into the time, locality, setting and concern of their authors. Judith Butler (2008) is an exception, with her examination of the two forewords by Sartre and Bhabha that are included in the new translation of Fanon's *Les damnés de la terre* by Richard Philcox (Fanon 2004).[2] Scrutinising Sartre's shifting use of pronominal address with an eye to revealing the implied reader in the Preface, Butler explores the 'question of the human to come' (Butler 2008, p. 218), 'violence' (2008, pp. 220–21) and 'psychoaffective survival' (2008, p. 221) from a feminist perspective. She touches on Bhabha's

Foreword, but her chief interest lies with Sartre and his problematic 'masculine' rapport with anticolonialism, a concern spurred by various current reprisals of Sartre's philosophy.

However, the reappraisal of Sartre's work and the reconsideration of Hegel's dialectic in the context of contemporary decolonial critical race studies invite a more extensive engagement with the forewords to Fanon's canonical text than Butler provides. Her deconstructionist reading, highlighting Sartre's apparently Hegel-inspired description of slavery as 'social death' (2008, p. 215), needs to be augmented by closer analysis of the Sartre and Bhabha paratexts and the extent to which they resonate with Hegelian dialectics. That is the task of my re-reading of the two forewords presented in this chapter. It will be guided by the following questions: by what cultural (discursive) dissemination and transaction did the forewords, separated by more than forty years, gain their salience? How do these forewords, and their authors, account for Fanon as an icon of anticolonial (Sartre), postcolonial (Bhabha) and decolonial thought after the decolonial turn? How are entwined questions of violence and freedom taken up? To what extent does a sense of Hegel's famous 'Herr-Knecht' ('lord–bondsman') dynamic underwrite the reception of the 1961 text? Does it continue to underlie what Gayatri Spivak (Spivak 1999, p. 172) calls 'postcoloniality – the contemporary global condition'?

Kojève and the Algerian War as intertext in Fanon and Sartre

In *Les damnés de la terre*, Fanon seems to condemn the impact of the 'master–slave' dynamic, invoking Hegel's definitive term 'spirit': 'The West [*L'Occident*] saw itself as a spiritual adventure [*une aventure de l'Esprit*]. It is in the name of the spirit, in the name of the spirit of Europe, that Europe has made her encroachments, that she has justified her crimes and legitimized the slavery [*l'esclavage*] in which she holds four-fifth of humanity' (Fanon [1961] 1967, p. 252, [1961] 2004, p. 237). Such an implicit rebuke of Hegelian dialectics of Reason and History attests to the immense influence exerted by Alexandre Kojève's

Marxist-inflected, proto-existentialist, Husserlian-inspired lectures on Hegel's *Phenomenology of the Spirit* (Kojève [1947] 1980). Between 1933 and 1939 Kojève conducted seminars at the École des Hautes Études in Paris that were 'regularly attended by leading figures of French intellectual life at that time, such as Georges Bataille, Jacques Lacan, André Breton, Maurice Merleau-Ponty and Raymond Aron' (Groys 2016, p. 29; see also Descombes 1982, p. 10 n. 1).[3] Though Sartre was not among the regular attendees, his erstwhile friend Merleau-Ponty, the founder of 'existential phenomenology' (Descombes 1982, p. 56) and one of Fanon's teachers at the University of Lyon, would have transmitted to Sartre the then popular ideas in the course of their joint work on the left-wing polemical journal *Les temps modernes* (published from 1945 onwards).

After Fanon's earlier disagreement with Sartre over the latter's initial support of *Négritude* extolled in *Présence Africaine* (Macey 2001, p.186; Sekyi-Otu 1996, pp. 16–17), Sartre and Fanon found themselves on the same side in their militant support for the Algerian struggle for independence, which was brutally repressed by French armed forces from 1954 to 1962. Sartre's Preface to *The Wretched of the Earth* testifies explicitly to this crucial event in French colonial history, referring to the terror engineered by the French secret service, the OAS (*Organisation armée secrète*), which the 'Grand Magician' (President de Gaulle) hides 'at all costs' but which 'bursts out at Metz' and elsewhere in metropolitan France (Sartre [1961] 1967, p. 24, [1961] 2004b, p. lxi). Decolonisation, for which Fanon had fought for more than a decade, had moved from the North African periphery to the heart of the colonial state, an event that has significantly troubled French historical memory ever since.[4]

Moral outrage at the oppression of the Muslim population in Algeria and the torture of captives by the French military had propelled Sartre to take sides in *Les temps modernes*.[5] His hostility towards the French Right and supporters of French Algeria (and of the actions of the OAS) had been met with explicit threats and even two bomb explosions at the entrance to his apartment building.[6] It would have come as no surprise, then, that by 1961 Sartre's vocal opposition to colonialism and its structural exploitation ([1961] 1967, p. 8, [1961] 2004b, p. xliv) had convinced Fanon to instruct his publisher, François Maspero, to invite Sartre to write a 'preface to *The Wretched of the Earth*' (Bernasconi 2010, p. 37), the book hastily completed before Fanon's untimely death in December 1961. When choosing 'his own book title' for the first time, Robert Bernasconi (2010, p. 42) suggests, Fanon might have had in mind the admired philosopher's *Critique of Dialectical Reason*, a book Fanon references in his first chapter, 'Concerning Violence' (Fanon [1961] 1967, p. 67, [1961] 2004, p. 43), in connection with the inevitable violent struggle for freedom. In the *Critique* Sartre characterises as *damned* those who are 'the least favoured', albeit with reference to the tension between skilled and unskilled workers (Bernasconi 2010, pp. 43, 46 n. 20).[7] However, with the title *Les damnés de la terre*, Fanon could have been alluding to a phrase Sartre had utilised to characterise the rural masses of the 'Third World' (Sartre [1960] 2004a: 241); it would have been yet another indication of the closeness of their thinking.[8]

Like Sartre's earlier existentialist writings, the *Critique* is unmistakably infused with Kojève-inflected Hegelianism, with its particular emphasis on the concept of negation and militant human struggle for recognition, the consciousness and lived experience of the 'slave', the claim to primacy of action over being, truth as revealed in and validated by 'the end of history', and what Sartre calls 'atheist humanism' (Descombes 1982, p. 29). Sartre glosses Fanon's statements in an attempt to amplify the call to overdue violent revolution that Fanon had addressed to the marginalised, colonised and oppressed, in short to those con-*damned* to silence. He picks passages from Fanon's text specially designed to show the underside of 'racist humanism' (Sartre [1961] 1967, p. 22, [1961] 2004b, p. lviii), such as the chapters 'Concerning Violence' (Fanon [1961] 1967, pp. 27–84, [1961] 2004, pp. 1–62) and 'Conclusion' ([1961] 1967, pp. 251–55, [1961] 2004, pp. 235–39) that frame the remaining four chapters, which were written earlier for different occasions. These two chapters in particular allow Sartre to telescope in parallel a modern post-Enlightenment history of the coloniser-colonised relation, by juxtaposing a 'First World' perspective (his own) with a 'native', 'Third World' one (that of Fanon).

Thus two divergent optics reinforce an identical mid-twentieth-century global demographic: Sartre's opening sentence of the Preface reads 'the earth [numbers] two thousand million inhabitants; five hundred million men, and one thousand five hundred million natives' (Sartre [1961] 1967, p. 7, [1961] 2004b, p. xliii); in Fanon's original formulation, 'four-fifths of humanity' had their slave status instituted and 'legitimized [in] the spirit of Europe' (Fanon [1961] 1967, p. 252, [1961] 2004, p. 236), amounting to 'the bloodless genocide which consisted in the setting aside of fifteen thousand millions of men' ([1961] 1967, p. 254, [1961] 2004, p. 238). These numbers provide proof for Sartre's claim that, whereas one fifth of the world's population 'had the word; the others had the use of it' (Sartre [1961] 1967, p. 7, [1961] 2004b, p. xliii). His comment highlights the corresponding epistemic injustice, prompting him to address the French settlers in Algeria: 'Europeans, you must open this book and enter into it' ([1961] 1967, p. 11, [1961] 2004b, p. xlviii). He implores them to listen to the excluded, silenced majority on whose behalf Fanon raises his voice while dismissing Western values, including *évolué* assimilatory aspirations obtained by mimicking a hollow civilisation void of ethical life: 'Let us waste no time in sterile litanies and nauseating mimicry. Leave this Europe where they are never done talking of Man, yet murder men everywhere they find them ... For centuries they have stifled almost the whole of humanity in the name of a so-called spiritual experience' (Fanon [1961] 1967, p. 251, [1961] 2004, p. 235). Fanon thus reveals the white man's civilisation as sham.

Universal rights and their racial exclusions: dialectical paralysis

Sartre repeats, and by such doubling maximises, Fanon's diagnostics (Fanon [1961] 1967, p. 8, also p. 251, [1961] 2004, p. xliv, also p. 234), so as to bring home the ugly reverse of the failed project of 'bourgeois humanist ideology' he had dismantled in *Critique of Dialectical Reason*

(Sartre [1960] 2004a, p. 753). To strengthen their shared anticolonialist stance, Sartre intersperses illuminating passages about the ravages of colonialist oppression with his own comments on the desperate political situation at a particular historical moment. He thus positions a colonised subject (the *évolué* Fanon) dialectically opposite a self-conscious coloniser (Sartre) who seems shamed by what he glosses. By these means, contemporary readers in 1961 are forced to see both sides of an adversarial colonial encounter, reflexively paired in (dialectically) antithetical positions. For an illustration of Sartre's critical (dialectical), double synchronic and diachronic movement mentioned earlier, I have arranged the two contrasting positions in parallel columns:

Fanon's diachronic 'panorama on three levels'	*Sartre's double synchronic and diachronic movement*
• At first there is assimilation to and correspondence with metropolitan literature (Fanon [1961] 1967, p. 178, [1961] 2004, p. 158).	• There was manufacture of 'a native *élite*' that had branded on their foreheads 'the principles of western culture' (Sartre [1961] 1967, p. 7, [1961] 2004b, p. xliii).
• This is followed by a return to 'past happenings of the bygone days', when the native's 'childhood will be brought up out of the depths of his memory' ([1961] 1967, p. 179, [1961] 2004, p. 159).	• '[Black] and yellow voices still spoke of our humanism but only to reproach us for our inhumanity' ([1961] 1967, p. 7, [1961] 2004b, p. xliii).
• And finally, the fighting phase produces a 'fighting literature, a revolutionary literature, and a national literature … which expresses the heart of the people' and strives 'to become the mouthpiece of a new reality', defining 'the epoch through which the people are treading out their path towards history' ([1961] 1967, p. 181, [1961] 2004, p. 162).	• A generation emerges that accuses its masters (here Sartre is quoting Fanon) of 'making us into monstrosities; your humanism claims we are at one with the rest of humanity but your racist methods set us apart' ([1961] 1967, p. 8, [1961] 2004b, p. xliv).

In the left column key thoughts from Fanon's temporalised (diachronic) 'panorama on three levels' in his chapter 'On National Culture' (Fanon [1961] 1967, p. 178, [1961] 2004, p. 158) are captured, while in the column on the right Sartre's Preface responds to Fanon's timeline by reflecting on 'three generations' (Sartre [1961] 1967, p. 14, [1961] 2004b, p. li). While the left column tells of the historical rise to self-consciousness reflected in, and coextensive with, particular forms of literary production (as evidenced elsewhere, among other instances, in *Présence Africaine*), the right column unmasks as false the rhetoric of 'humanism claims' experienced by the *évolué* Fanon (Sartre [1961] 2004b, p. xix) in being stereotyped by 'the gaze of racist recognition', during his studies in Lyon. Unlike what pertained in the colonies and in Martinique, the standard of social acceptance in Lyon was not 'foremost determined by class and language' (Ehlen 2000, p. 27), but by race.[9]

Fanon denounces the failure of the (modern) colonial state to fully integrate the *évolué* into French society as the equal citizen he is *'de jure'* but not in praxis (Fanon [1961] 1967, p. 21, [1961] 2004, p. lviii). With bitter irony Sartre, from the opposite position, denounces the betrayal of 'the principles of western culture' (Sartre [1961] 1967, p. 7, [1961] 2004b, p. xliii) embodied in the rights that the French Revolution has come to represent.[10] Thus, the French political tradition sees rights as universal, and as natural benefits of being human; 'race', as a putatively negative component of social life, had become an issue only in the nineteenth century. To Sartre's consternation, the Europeans, despite their professed revolutionary ideals, are deeply complicit with colonialism. With left liberals being no exception, they continue to assert leadership of the civilised, moral world (Sartre [1961] 1967, p. 12, [1961] 2004b, p. xlviii) that Fanon diagnoses as stagnant: 'Today we are present at the stasis of Europe. Comrades, let us flee from this motionless movement where gradually dialectic is changing into the logic of equilibrium. Let us reconsider the question of *mankind*. Let us reconsider the question of cerebral reality and the cerebral mass of all humanity, whose connections must be increased, whose channels must be diversified and whose messages must be re-humanized' (Fanon [1961] 1967, p. 253, [1961] 2004, p. 237). Although Fanon's and Sartre's positions concerning dialectical paralysis converge, there can be no doubt about the existence of an unbridgeable chasm between master and slave, coloniser and racialised colonised, as indicated in the content of the comparison on page 123.

In terms of Hegel's Enlightenment idea of perfectibility through human culture (*Bildung*), along a progressively emancipatory trajectory – as summarised in the right-hand column from the opening pages of Sartre's Preface – the 'native brought into existence by the settler', as Fanon expresses it (Fanon [1961] 1967, p. 28, [1961] 2004, p. 2), should have been fully assimilated 'with the rest of humanity' in all aspects of his existence, including Kojévean-Hegelian universal history. But for Fanon, 'Western bourgeois racial prejudice as regards the nigger and the Arab as a racism of contempt' ([1961] 1967, p. 131, [1961] 2004, p. 110) prevent 'people' fashioned as 'monstrosities' from gaining their rightful place in history, even though the 'people' have successfully advanced from 'native' (single being) to collaborative *praxis* of 'the people' – a progression that has empowered the 'people' to 'tread ... out their path towards history'. This is a path in line with the one that Sartre traces in his *Critique of Dialectical Reason* as a process of the human's dialectical self-development from inert 'seriality' to collective praxis. It is a path that should have been open to the 'colonial subjects as children' who, in the words of Paul Reynaud, the Minister of Colonies in 1931, under the tutelage of France, 'their generous mother' (as cited in Cohen 1970, p. 427), would have acquired the language required for entering the metropolitan First World.[11] But 'racist methods' like those experienced by the *évolué* Fanon prevented the successful achievement of the *mission civilisatrice* as outlined in ministerial thinking, as Fanon wryly observes throughout *The Wretched of the Earth*.

However, a 'Manichean opposition between the putative superiority of the European and the supposed inferiority of the native' (JanMohamed 1985, p. 63), exasperated by 'race as "the *differentia specifica"'* (Sekyi-Otu 1996, p. 13) under conditions of colonialism, with its corollary of political oppression and economic exploitation, cannot but harbour seeds of rebellion. In the next section I will turn to a consideration of this rebellious potential, and its activation.

'Let us burst into history'

Given that the natives are twice con-*damned*, as *nègre* and as slave, by the inherent violence of bourgeois respectability that Sartre's *Critique of Dialectical Reason* consistently attacks, it is no wonder that they have no other choice than to free themselves from the master's norm-dictating stranglehold. 'Let us burst into history, forcing it by our invasion into universality for the first time', Fanon, quoted by Sartre (Sartre [1961] 1967, p. 11, [1961] 2004b, p. xlviii), urges his fellow *damned*, at a crucial (historical) instant when rival factions have produced 'paralysis' during the battle for Algeria: 'Let us start fighting; and if we've no other arms, the waiting knife's enough.' Fanon calls for 'the liberation of the national territory' and 'a continual struggle against colonialism' (Fanon [1961] 1967, p. 189, [1961] 2004, p. 170), echoing Kojève's claim (Kojève [1947] 1980, p. 9) that human culture emerges from the life and consciousness of the slave, and that it is the slave who makes history.

In similar vein, Sartre supports Fanon's claims (Fanon [1961] 1967, p. 40, [1961] 2004, p. 14) that 'in the past we made history and now it is being made of us. The ratio of forces has been inverted; decolonization has begun; all that our hired soldiers [in Algeria] can do is to delay its completion' (Sartre [1961] 1967, p. 23, [1961] 2004b, p. lx). Even if 'colonial administrators' did not 'read Hegel', Sartre opines ([1961] 1967, p. 8, [1961] 2004b, p. xliv), 'they do not need a philosopher to tell them that uneasy consciences are caught up in their own contradictions' inherent in the civilisatory mission.[12] 'Our methods are out-of-date,' he concludes, 'they can sometimes delay emancipation, but not stop it' ([1961] 1967, p. 11, [1961] 2004b, p. xlvii). Armed with the logic of negation, he exposes the 'contradiction' that arises from '[laying] claim to and denying [the natives] the human condition at the same time' ([1961] 1967, p. 17,

[1961] 2004b, p. liv). Whereas the realisation of the flawed – because deceptively executed – Hegelian project of development prompts Sartre, as mentioned previously, to implore French settlers in Algeria to 'open this book and enter into it' so as to understand the historic situation (Sartre [1961] 1967, p. 11, [1961] 2004b, p. xlviii), Fanon regards the 'book' as a manifesto for the 'war of liberation' (Fanon [1961] 1967, p. 108, [1961] 2004, p. 86) that clinches the 'struggle for freedom' ([1961] 1967, p. 45, [1961] 2004, p. 20), coeval with a rejection of 'the stasis of Europe' and 'the logic of equilibrium' ([1961] 1967, p. 253, [1961] 2004, p. 237). For Sartre, the time has come to instantiate 'the end of the dialectic' (*le dernier moment*') and to 'join the ranks of those [the colonized] who make history' (Sartre [1961] 1967, p. 26, [1961] 2004b, p. lxxii).[13]

Thus, two contrary positions occupied by the coloniser and the colonised are locked in reciprocal exclusion that is made manifest in enforced geographic segregation (Fanon [1961] 1967, pp. 29–31, [1961] 2004, pp. 3–5). For Fanon, '[two] zones are opposed, but not in service of a higher unity. Obedient to the rules of pure Aristotelian logic, they both follow the principle of reciprocal exclusivity' ([1961] 1967, p. 30, [1961] 2004, p. 4; see also chapter one by Ato Sekyi-Otu in this book). The French original (Fanon 2002, p. 42) more accurately captures the sense of Hegelian thought expressed as '*Wechselwirkung*' (reciprocal efficacy), as for instance in Hegel ([1807] 1973, p. 329 – §§330, 331): '*Régies par une logique purement aristotélicienne, elles obéissent au principe d'exclusion réciproque: il n'y a pas de conciliation possible ...*' ('governed by a purely Aristotelian logic, they obey the principle of reciprocal exclusion: there is no possible conciliation'); that is why the 'end of the dialectic' has been reached. For a dialectical (analytical) resolution requires a meditative step to overcome negation ('exclusivity') in a sublatory ('*aufgehobene*') 'higher unity' or synthesis. Failing to include this step can, in Hegel's words, result only in 'cold annihilation' (Hegel [1807] 1977, p. 360 – §591) or, in respect of the Algerian situation, in 'armed combat' (Fanon [1961] 1967, p. 237, [1961] 2004, p. 219). 'The colonized races, those slaves of modern times, are impatient', Fanon warns ([1961] 1967,

p. 58, [1961] 2004, p. 34). They threaten to explode a Manichaean logic, or what amounts to a restricted dialectic frozen in 'stasis', especially when colonialism becomes compounded by the notion of 'race', absent in Hegel.[14] Not surprisingly, Fanon claims repeatedly that 'the colonial world is a Manichaean world' ([1961] 1967, p. 31, [1961] 2004, p. 6), adding in a footnote that he has 'demonstrated its mechanism' in *Black Skin, White Masks* ([1961] 1967, p. 32 n., [1961] 2004, p. 6 n. 1).

Hegel's dialectic versus colonial Manichaeism

In contrast to Hegel's analytic, the economy of the 'Manichaeistic world' (Fanon [1961] 1967, p. 40, [1961] 2004, p. 15) represents an adversarial, irreconcilable duality; this duality cannot lead to the synthesis of a difference that is itself differential, because Manichaeism imperils Hegel's tripartite dialectic of Reason (sense-certainty, perception and finally understanding) by reducing it to an antithetical paralysis mired in differing ascriptions of value.[15] For Manichaeism is less a *logical* structure of *antithetical positions* than an *axiological* structure of *adversarial positioning* along a moral/ethical spectrum. In the ensuing competition over values, there is no middle ground and hence no reconciliation. For Fanon's Kojève/Sartre-inflected thought, there is thus in the 'struggle for recognition' no alignment through mediation to reconciliation and synthesis, but only combat to the death (see chapter two in this book by Philippe Van Haute on the theoretical role of violence in Fanon); this is evident in the history of the religious movement of the same name, and is replayed in the colonial racism thematised in *The Wretched* [the damned] *of the Earth*.[16]

For Fanon, Manichaeism inheres in 'the white man's values' ([1961] 1967, pp. 33–34, [1961] 2004, p. 8), articulated in the colonial world in the dichotomous relation between colonised/'slave' and settler/'master'. Once the colonised stubbornly refuses, in Sartre's words, 'the animal condition' (Sartre [1961] 1967, p. 15, [1961] 2004b, p. lii) provided in 'the bestiary' that, in Fanon's view, is allotted to him by Europeans (Fanon [1961] 1967, p. 33, [1961] 2004, p. 7), violence is pervasive insofar as it 'has ruled over the ordering of the colonial worlds', as Fanon claims ([1961] 1967, p. 31, [1961] 2004, p. 5).[17] His diagnosis of a Manichaean world as one 'bisected into economically and racially defined compartments, a world cut in two' and 'inhabited by two different species' ([1961] 1967, p. 3, [1961] 2004, p. 5) resonates with Sartre's. In the *Critique of Dialectical Reason* (Sartre [1960] 2004a, p. 733), Sartre urges the colonial world to 'confront', at the juncture between opposing forces, 'total negation with total negation, violence with equal violence' for 'the violence of the rebel *was* the violence of the colonialist; there were never any other'. Fanon concurs: 'Manichaeism of the settler produces a Manichaeism of the native. To the theory of the "absolute evil of the native" the theory of the "absolute evil of the settler" replies' (Fanon [1961] 1967, p. 73, [1961] 2004, p. 30).[18] What is more, Fanon states unequivocally that 'Manichaeism goes to its logical conclusion and dehumanizes the native, or to speak plainly it turns him into an animal' ([1961] 1967, p. 32, [1961] 2004, p. 7).[19] The same sentiment is borne out in Sartre's earlier accounts of French perceptions of Muslim fighters in Algeria, in his *Critique of Dialectical Reason* (Sartre [1960] 2004a, p. 715): 'They were either "devils" or "mindless savages", depending whether they had won a victory, showing them in their *activity* or whether, on the contrary, they had suffered a temporary defeat, which is in itself an affirmation of the conqueror's superiority. In either case, this Manichaean action, separating the hostile troops by the absolute negation of a line of fire, makes the Muslim *other than man'*.

A restricted dialectic in the form of Manichaeism invites resolution by the annihilation of colonial regimes and their attendant administrations, or at least, for Fanon, by 'armed struggle' against the oppressor. At this critical juncture, Fanon applies Hegel's idea of 'unity' (Fanon [1961] 1967, p. 73; translated as 'totalizing' in [1961] 2004, p. 50) to the empirical situation whereby the oppressed groups, bound together 'in the great organism of violence which has surged upwards in reaction to the settler's violence', might bring about reciprocal 'recognition' in each of the group's members, thus assuring the future nation's indivisibility

([1961] 1967, p. 73, [1961] 2004, p. 50). However, such a truncated dialectic, with its rejection of reconciliation, cannot but produce 'retributive violence' (Bhabha 2004, p. xxxviii); in line with Manichaean combat, the 'development of violence among the colonized people will be proportionate to the violence exercised by the threatened colonial regime', as Fanon warns prophetically (Fanon [1961] 1967, p. 69, [1961] 2004, p. 46) – a vision incisively endorsed in Sartre's anticolonialist Preface. Hence the violence that, in Bhabha's words (Bhabha 2004, p. xxi), became the *cause célèbre* of the first chapter' of *The Wretched of the Earth*. It is to Bhabha's reading of this work that I now turn.

On the question of violence: Bhabha obscuring Hegel

In his 1994 essay on Fanon, 'Interrogating Identity: Frantz Fanon and the Postcolonial Prerogative', Bhabha misreads Fanon's clear-eyed statement on the Manichaean colonial world: 'Unlike Fanon I think the *non-dialectical moment* of Manichaeism suggests an answer. By following the trajectory of colonial desire ... it becomes possible to cross, even to shift the Manichaean boundaries' (Bhabha 1994a, p. 62). But is it not precisely the 'Manichean and physically grounded stalemate Fanon's entire work follows' that makes violence the 'force intended to bridge the gap between white and non-white', as Edward Said argues (Said 1994, p. 326)? Violence for Fanon, Said continues, 'is the synthesis that overcomes the reification of white man as subject, Black man as object' (1994, p. 326). Bhabha concludes (Bhabha 2004, p. xl, citing Fanon [1961] 2004, p. 44), that 'violence can thus be understood to be the perfect mediation [*la médiation royale* in the French original]. The colonized man liberates himself in and through violence. This praxis enlightens the militant because it shows him the means and the end. Césaire's poetry takes on a prophetic significance in this very prospect of violence.'

For emphasis, Bhabha later adds a further quote from Fanon to capture 'the tone of those apocalyptic times' in the early 1960s (Bhabha 2004, p. xxxv): 'The colonized subject discovers reality and transforms it through his praxis, his deployment of violence and his agenda for liberation' (Fanon [1961] 2004, p. 21; see also Beata Stawarska's analysis of the affirmative role of violence for Simone de Beauvoir and Fanon in chapter five of this book). Violence as Manichean tool par excellence might furnish the royal road to liberation as happened after Fanon's death, but what about a postcolonial world? How will an instrumental 'means-end' logic driving liberation movements face political praxis in the new, decolonised state? Bhabha (2004, p. xxxvi) mentions Hannah Arendt's concern over 'the death of politics'. It will be remembered that Arendt, in her political-philosophical investigation of violence, rejects it vehemently (Arendt 1969, p. 149) as a foundation for a working politics. Yet the question of the political, not glossed by Sartre, becomes rightly imperative for Bhabha, who in his Foreword twice underwrites Fanon's assertion (Fanon [1961] 2004, p. 40) that 'the colonized, underdeveloped man is a political creature in the most global sense of the term' (Bhabha 2004, pp. vii, xi). However, the centrality of this assertion envisioning, after postcolonialism, a decolonial body politic speaks far more clearly from Constance Farrington's translation of the original than from Philcox cited above. For Farrington conveys Fanon's Hegelian-inspired sense more accurately in her wording: 'the native and the underdeveloped man are today *political animals* in the most *universal sense* of the word' (Fanon [1961] 1967, p. 64, emphasis added), since the Aristotelian connotation attached to '*animaux politiques*' (Fanon [1961] 2002, p. 79), together with the phrase 'universal sense', speak in the Kojèvian language of the *Phenomenology* ignored by Bhabha. It is the language of a more encompassing promise of political (Aristotelian) and universal (Hegelian) acumen on the part of Third World actors whose once muted voices are now clearly audible, seeking control of their narrative.

Though Bhabha is cognisant of Fanon's (instrumental) '*violence, dans son projet de liberation*' ('violence for the purpose of his [the colonized's] liberation') (Fanon [1961] 2002: 59), his Foreword (Bhabha 2004, pp. vii–xli) skirts the topic of violence beyond acknowledging its somewhat dated objective, which stemmed from 'violence and counterviolence' forged in 'these [Algerian War] conditions of dire extremity' (Bhabha 2004, p. xxxiv).[20] He merely references the exasperation expressed by Fanon's widow, Josie Fanon, at yet another Algerian rebellion in 1988 – 'Oh Frantz, the wretched of the earth again'[21] – before proposing 'a different reading of Fanonian violence [as] part of the struggle for psycho-affective survival and search for human agency in the midst of the agony of oppression' (2004, p. xxxvii).[22] It is this type of reading, defined by what Macey (2001, p. 27) disparagingly calls a 'post-colonial theorist's enthusiasm for Derrida and Lacan', that also characterises Bhabha's earlier engagements with Fanon in the Foreword to the 1986 edition of *Black Skin, White Masks* (Bhabha 1986, pp. xxi–xxxviii) and its near copy, 'Interrogating Identity' (Bhabha 1994a). In the eyes of Bhabha (1986, p. xxiii), Fanon's body of work 'splits between a Hegelian–Marxist dialectic, a phenomenological affirmation of Self and Other and the psychoanalytic ambivalence of the Unconscious, its turning from love to hate, mastery to servitude' whereby 'his Hegelianism restores hope to history; his existentialist evocation of the "I" restores the presence of the marginalized; and his psychoanalytic framework illuminates the "madness" of racism, the pleasure of pain, the agonistic fantasy of political power'.[23] But despite the nod to Hegel (and by implication to Sartre and Lacan), Bhabha's analyses remain staunchly resistant to the consistent linear formulation that made Hegel's dialectic, and with it the grand logical and historical narratives of the 'new man', so suspect for postcolonial theory.

Typically, the key term most used in Bhabha's deconstructivist reading of *The Wretched of the Earth* is 'psycho-affective'. He states, for example: 'I want to argue that the troubled traffic between the psychic body and the body politic – the subjective experience of objective reality so typical of Fanon's style – suggests that the psycho-affective relation is also "the glowing focal point where citizen and individual develop and grow"' (Bhabha 2004, p. xxi, citing Fanon [1961] 2004, p. 4). Thus, Bhabha maps Fanon's biographical and historical experience across a changed global landscape by focusing on its economic, cultural and psychological maladies. In this way, according to him, Fanon's 'critical imagination' (Sekyi-Otu 2003) transcribes the master–slave antagonisms into problems between a wealthy metropolis and 'the dispossessed wretched of the earth' (Bhabha 2004, p. xxviii; Macey 2001, p. 6), suggesting similarities between the compartmentalised colonial world and the margins, and between the industrialised regions of a global world and the 'underdeveloped' Third World.

Concerned about the world-wide 'legacy of Fanon' (Bhabha 2004, p. x) after the end of the Cold War, Bhabha catalogues at length the political protests inspired by empathy with the rage against colonialism expressed by Fanon and Sartre (2004: xxviii–xxxi).[24] Eager to render relevant a book 'coming to us from the distances of mid-century decolonization', he examines 'Fanon's demand for a fair distribution of rights and resources', judging it to be 'a timely intervention in a decade-long debate on social equity that has focused perhaps too exclusively on the [very North American] culture wars, the politics of identity, and the politics of recognition' (2004, p. xviii). According to Bibhash Choudhury (2016, p. 184), Bhabha's 'culturalisation' takes Fanon's critical work out of philosophy into the burgeoning field of postcolonialism. Quoting Bhabha from *The Location of Culture* (Bhabha 1994b, pp. 245–46), Choudhury sees postcolonial criticism as undertaking 'critical revisions around issues of cultural difference, social authority, and political discrimination in order to reveal the antagonistic and ambivalent moments within the "rationalizations" of modernity' (Choudhury 2016, p. 183).[25]

Remnants of Hegel after Sartre's and Bhabha's readings of *The Wretched of the Earth*

No doubt, Sartre's Preface and Bhabha's Foreword contour two different pathways to *The Wretched of the Earth*. In sharp contrast with Bhabha, the referential framework for Sartre's Fanon reading is unmistakably Kojève-Hegelian. Unflinchingly committed to anticolonialism, Sartre's Preface, particularly in the Farrington translation, made Fanon's clarion call for the independence of Algeria palpable for European audiences in the 1960s. But a vastly changed historical context, not to mention a millennial Anglo-American readership, account for Bhabha's consciously un-Hegelian, postcolonial assessment. Moreover, the new Philcox translation largely erases intertextual allusions to Hegelianism in Fanon's and Sartre's original French texts. Arguably, their fierce anticolonial stance helped give birth to decolonial, or rather postcolonial, thinking in what has become known as 'writing back' on the part of formerly colonised subjects, chief among them Bhabha. Postcolonial thought continues to uphold Fanon's, by now canonised, text as a (re)source for ongoing debates in and about the space inhabited by 'the emerging African subject' (Mbembe 2001, p. 15), a space Achille Mbembe (2001) calls the 'postcolony', where the effects of colonisation on the colonised – the 'wretched' or rather 'condemned of the earth' – live the legacy of colonialism. There, questions of knowledge and reasoning with Hegel outside Kojève's interpretation of the *Phenomenology* must remain relevant.

However, typically decolonial epistemic questions of content and the legitimising of what counts as worth knowing require exploration elsewhere. They are beyond the scope of my present concern with a truncated Hegelian dialectic and ominous Manichean axiology. It will be up to emerging readers and thinkers to revive the philosophical dialogue with Hegel proper, after having 'entered history' (Sartre-Fanon) and having gained political independence (Bhabha-Fanon) in the postcolony. But the looming danger of Manichaeism attendant on a restricted Hegelian analytic needs to be averted. For 'an inverted Manichaeism', one based on geography and race, for instance, tacitly disavows the complex political determinations that are central to the emancipatory politics it seeks to actualise (Vázquez-Arroyo 2018, p. 328). The warning voiced by Sekyi-Otu (2003) remains to be heeded: 'After Fanon, African criticism cannot feign ignorance of history. But neither can [it] plead captivity to its consequences' (Sekyi-Otu 2003, n.p.).

Notes

1   This is Gérard Genette's (1997, p. xi) term for a family of texts such as forewords, epigraphs, titles, dedications, and so on, which mediate the relations between the reader and the text that they introduce.

2   The 2004 translation by Richard Philcox of *Les damnés de la terre* features Bhabha's Foreword (Fanon 2004, pp. vii–xli), followed by Sartre's retranslated Preface to the French edition of 1961, originally translated by Constance Farrington ([1961] 1967, pp. 7–26, [1961] 2004b, pp. xliii–lxii). Despite the shortcomings of the Farrington translation (see Macey 2001, p. 26; also Batchelor 2017, pp. 45–47), I prefer to quote from it rather than from the Philcox translation, which tends to smother Fanon's and Sartre's Hegelian-induced thought praxis in sanitised rhetoric tailored for a postcolonial readership averse to violence. The significant interpretative conundrum arising from Philcox's new translation needs to be dealt with elsewhere.

3   In a recently published study, *The Black Circle: A Life of Alexandre Kojève*, Jeff Love (2018) assesses the influential French-Russian transmitter and disseminator of Hegel and suggests that Kojève's Marxist-inspired interpretation of the *Phenomenology* ought to be read as 'narrative' rather than 'interpretation', particularly in light of the imbalance of Kojève's commentary that is 'almost wholly focused on two short chapters in the *Phenomenology*' (Love 2018, p.106), with an overwhelming focus on 'the master and slave' and 'the sage' (2018, p. 105).

4   The fraught memories of enemy participants in the Algerian conflict living in France prevented a revisiting of its history until very recently, and the conflict is mentioned only cursorily in the anglophone Fanon literature (with the exception of Macey 2001, pp. 493–98), references in Sartre's Preface notwithstanding.

5   In her book *Adieux: A Farewell to Sartre*, Simone de Beauvoir quotes the words of her life-long companion: 'I've always looked upon colonialism as an action of pure theft, the brutal conquest of a country and the absolutely intolerable exploitation of one country by another; I thought that all the colonial states should have to get rid of their colonies sooner or later' (Beauvoir 1985, p. 367). Similar claims are made at length in Sartre's *Critique of Dialectical Reason* ([1960] 2004a, pp. 714–34), where the liberation struggle between Muslims, French settlers in Algeria and the French army is debated at length.

6   A photograph of the damage done to the building is reproduced in Biemel (1990, p. 154).

7   I use the italicised terms *'damned'* and *'con-damned'* throughout this chapter to emphasise the notion of *damned* as far more telling than the weak

English translation 'wretched' used for '*damnés*' in both Fanon's and Sartre's parlance.

8   Bernasconi (2010, p. 44) credits George Ciccariello-Maher with identifying Sartre as the source for the title and Fanon as the spokesperson for *les damnés*, 'the damned'. It remains unclear, though, why the semantics of the original French title, which connote moral rejection with resultant condemnation of the colonised by the colonisers, should have been translated into English as 'wretched', a term that would correspond to *misérable* in French. The choice of title for the English translation – Farrington suggested 'The Rising of the Damned' (Batchelor 2017, p. 48) – together with the story of the book's reception in the anglophone world in contrast to the francophone world requires further research beyond Kathryn Batchelor's insightful treatment.

9   This, at any rate, is how Ehlen (2000, p. 89) interprets Fanon's famous statement, 'not a new man ... has come in, but a new kind of man, a new genus. Why, it's a Negro!'

10   The *Declaration of the Rights of Man*, usually seen as a pinnacle of Western culture, includes also the abolition of slavery for all French territories, although it was introduced again briefly by Napoleon. Thus, any reference to slaves and slavery in Sartre and Fanon can only be metaphorical.

11   The view of the indigene as a child was a widespread one. The influential French colonial journal, *L'Afrique francaise*, spoke in 1901 of the need to treat the African as a child. He was to be taught his duties, to accept French authority, and to be kept under control. Sartre alludes to this state of affairs with his reference to 'colonial administrators ... not paid to read Hegel' ([1961] 1967, p. 8, [1961] 2004b, p. xliv).

12   In mentioning 'self-contradictory postulations', Hegel was quite aware of this danger (Hegel [1807] 1977, p. 439 – §623).

13   Philcox ([1961] 2004b, p. lxxii) translates the French original, '*C'est le dernier moment de la dialectique*' more faithfully as 'This is the last stage of the dialectic'. However, Fanon's complete sentence is: '*C'est le dernier moment de la dialectique: vous condamnez cette guerre mais n'osez pas encore vous déclarer solidaires des combattants algériens; n'ayez crainte, comptez sur les colons et sur les mercenaires*' ('This is the last stage of the dialectic: you condemn this war but do not yet dare to declare your solidarity with the Algerian fighters; fear not, count on the settlers and mercenaries') (Fanon [1961] 2002, p. 38).

14   It should be noted with respect to Hegel's anatomy that it knows of no racial division. Discussing Fanon's utilisation of Hegel's *Phenomenology* in *Black Skin, White Masks*, Honenberger (2007, p. 161, n. 23) notes: 'It would ... be wrong to suppose that Fanon's reading of the Hegelian Master–Slave dialectic imputes racism to the dialectic itself considered as a theoretical artifact.

Fanon's primary point about the Hegelian Master–Slave dialectic is only that it is not *sufficient* to fully describe the relevant features of the colonial situation'.

15   In connection with what I call a tripartite dialectic, see John Niemeyer Findlay's explanation in his Introduction to A.V. Miller's translation of the *Phenomenology* (Hegel [1807] 1977, p. 15).

16   According to Henry Neumann (1919, p. 493), the third-century prophet Mani (or Manichaeus) believed in a 'sun-god' who had engendered a 'cosmic conflict between relatively equi-potent principles', thus turning the world into a perpetual conflict zone. There 'the perceptual opposition between light and dark took on the value of good and evil'; this is a value easily transferable to Fanon's notion of a racialised world, with its antagonistic division of humanity based on a subject's 'epidermalization – of this inferiority', discussed at length in *Black Skin, White Masks* (Fanon [1952] 1986, p. 4).

17   What needs to be noted in this context is the underlying *mis*-reading of Hegel's philosophy of nature by Kojève ([1947] 1980, p. 254), who equates the first step of the dialectical analytic, 'sense certainty', with empirical animal existence (for example Fanon's 'monstrosity' quoted earlier; see also chapter two by Philippe van Haute and chapter four by Josias Tembo in this book). Importantly, Sartre, in the *Critique of Dialectical Reason* (Sartre [1960] 2004a, pp. 110–11) defines the notion 'animal' in relation to oppression: 'it consists, rather, in treating the Other as animal … the slave acquires his animality, through the master, only after his humanity has been recognised … This is the contradiction of racism, colonialism, and all forms of tyranny: in order to treat a man like a dog, one must first recognise him as a man'.

18   Importantly, as Nigel Gibson and Roberto Beneduce claim, violence for the psychiatrist and nuanced thinker Fanon was always 'a problematic' (Gibson and Beneduce 2017, p. 7) in 'reaction to asymmetrical colonial violence' (2017, p. 8). It was not the necessary condition for 'the birthing of a new kind of human being', as is often assumed (2017, p. 6).

19   See also Achille Mbembe's Kojève-inspired notion, attributed to Hegel, of defeated consciousness as animal, discussed by Josias Tembo in chapter four of this book.

20   Fanon 'came to be seen as the apostle of violence', a misunderstanding that Macey imputes also to Arendt (Macey 2001, pp. 22–23). Macey (2001 pp. 474–87) discusses the topic of violence at length, arguing that Sartre's *Critique of Reason* apparently supplied 'the framework for description of violence for Fanon' (2001 p. 478). Roberts (2004, p. 143) adds that in 'the Sartre of the *Critique*, violence ensues in order to overcome mankind's alienation resulting from the phenomenological lived reality of scarcity in modern capitalist society'.

21 See in this regard the important information Macey (2001, p. 502) supplies concerning the National Liberation Front's 'corruption and stagnation', and Josie Fanon's suicide in 1989.

22 See Gibson and Beneduce (2017, p. 233) who, quoting Bhabha, strongly endorse the latter's 'discussion of anticolonial violence' in psychoanalytic terms.

23 See also Robert Young's assessment in *White Mythologies* (1990).

24 Having explored the issue at length, Kathryn Batchelor (2017, p. 68) concludes that Bhabha's assertion that Fanon's 'incendiary spirit' had 'set alight IRA [Irish Republican Army] passions' is completely erroneous.

25 But as Fredric Jameson points out in his Foreword to the 2004 edition of Sartre's *Critique of Dialectical Reason* (Jameson 2004, p. xiv), there might have been no need, in these 'rationalizations', to 'philosophize history'; yet 'the most tenacious' of the grand narratives, 'the story of modernization ... continues to have a powerful grip on political thinking East and West alike', despite postmodernist revisions.

References

Arendt, Hannah (1969). 'On violence'. In Hannah Arendt, *Crises of the Republic*. New York: Harcourt Brace Jovanovich.

Batchelor, Kathryn (2017). 'The translation of *Les Damnés de la Terre* into English: Exploring Irish connections'. In Kathryn Batchelor and Sue-Ann Harding (eds), *Translating Frantz Fanon Across Continents and Languages*. New York and Abingdon: Routledge.

Beauvoir, Simone de (1985). *Adieux: A Farewell to Sartre*. Translated by Patrick O'Brian. Harmondsworth: Penguin.

Bernasconi, Robert (2010). 'Fanon's *The Wretched of the Earth* as the fulfillment of Sartre's *Critique of Dialectical Reason*'. *Sartre Studies International* 16(2): 36–46.

Bhabha, Homi K. (1986). 'Foreword: Remembering Fanon: Self, Psyche and the Colonial Condition'. In Frantz Fanon, *Black Skin, White Masks*. Translated by Charles Lam Markmann. London: Pluto Press.

Bhabha, Homi K. (1994a). 'Interrogating identity: Frantz Fanon and the postcolonial prerogative'. In Homi K. Bhabha, *The Location of Culture*. London and New York: Routledge.

Bhabha, Homi K. (1994b). *The Location of Culture*. London and New York: Routledge.

Bhabha, Homi K. (2004). 'Foreword: Framing Fanon'. In Frantz Fanon, *The Wretched of the Earth*. Translated by Richard Philcox. New York: Grove Press.

Biemel, Walter (1990). *Sartre*. Reinbek: Rowohlt.

Butler, Judith (2008). 'Violence, non-violence: Sartre on Fanon'. In Jonathan Judaken (ed.), *Race after Sartre: Antiracism, Africana Existentialism, Postcolonialism*. Albany: State of New York University Press.

Choudhury, Bibhash (2016). *Reading Postcolonial Theory: Key Texts in Context*. Abingdon and New York: Routledge.

Cohen, William B. (1970). 'The colonized as child: British and French colonial rule'. *African Historical Studies* 3(2): 427–31.

Descombes, Vincent (1982). *Modern French Philosophy*. Translated by Lorna Scott-Fox and Juliana M. Harding. Cambridge: Cambridge University Press.

Ehlen, Patrick (2000). *Frantz Fanon: A Spiritual Biography*. New York: Crossroad Publishing Company.

Fanon, Frantz (1967). *The Wretched of the Earth* (1961). Translated by Constance Farrington. Harmondsworth: Penguin.

Fanon, Frantz (1986). *Black Skin, White Masks* (1952). Translated by Charles Lam Markmann. London: Pluto Press.

Fanon, Frantz (2002). *Les damnés de la terre* (1961). Paris: Découverte Poche.

Fanon, Frantz (2004). *The Wretched of the Earth* (1961). Translated by Richard Philcox. New York: Grove Press.

Genette, Gérard (1997). *Paratexts: Thresholds of Interpretation*. Translated by Jane E. Lewin. Cambridge: Cambridge University Press.

Gibson, Nigel C. and Beneduce, Roberto (2017). *Frantz Fanon, Psychiatry and Politics*. London and New York: Rowan and Littlefield.

Groys, Boris (2016). 'Romantic bureaucracy: Alexandre Kojève's post-historical wisdom'. *Radical Philosophy* 196: 29–38.

Hegel, Georg Wilhelm Friedrich (1973). *Phänomenolgie des Geistes* (1807). Texte-Auswahl und Kommentar zur Rezeptionsgeschichte von Gerhard Göhler. Frankfurt/Main: Ullstein.

Hegel, Georg Wilhelm Friedrich (1977). *Hegel's Phenomenology of Spirit* (1807). Translated by A.V. Miller. Oxford: Clarendon Press.

Honenberger, Phillip (2007). '"Le Nègre et Hegel": Fanon on Hegel, colonialism, and the dialectics of recognition'. *Human Architecture: Journal of the Sociology of Self-Knowledge* 5(3): 153–62.

Jameson, Fredric (2004). 'Foreword'. In Jean-Paul Sartre, *Critique of Dialectical Reason*, vol. 1: *Theory of Practical Ensembles*. Translated by Alan Sheridan-Smith, edited by Jonathan Rée. London: Verso.

JanMohamed, Abdul R. (1985). 'The economy of Manichean allegory: The function of racial difference in colonialist literature'. *Critical Inquiry* 12(1): 59–87.

Kojève, Alexandre (1980). *Introduction to the Reading of Hegel: Lectures on the Phenomenology of Spirit* (1947). Assembled by Raymond Queneau, edited by Allan Bloom, translated by James H. Nichols Jr. Ithaca: Cornell University Press.

Love, Jeff (2018). 'The last revolution'. In Jeff Love, *The Black Circle: A Life of Alexandre Kojève*. New York: Columbia University Press.

Macey, David (2001). *Frantz Fanon: A Biography*. New York: Picador.

Mbembe, Achille (2001). *On the Postcolony*. Berkeley: University of California Press.

Neumann, Henry (1919). 'Manichaean tendencies in the history of philosophy'. *The Philosophical Review* 28(5): 491–510.

Roberts, Neil (2004). 'Fanon, Sartre, violence, and freedom'. *Sartre Studies International* 10(2): 139–60.

Said, Edward W. (1994). *Culture and Imperialism*. London: Vintage.

Sartre, Jean-Paul (1961). 'Préface à l'édition de 1961'. In Frantz Fanon, *Les damnés de la terre*. Paris: Découverte Poche.

Sartre, Jean-Paul (1967). 'Preface' (1961). In Frantz Fanon, *The Wretched of the Earth*. Translated by Constance Farrington. Harmondsworth: Penguin.

Sartre, Jean-Paul (2004a). *Critique of Dialectical Reason* (1960). Translated by Alan Sheridan-Smith, edited by Jonathan Rée. London: NLB.

Sartre, Jean-Paul (2004b). 'Preface' (1961). In Frantz Fanon, *The Wretched of the Earth*. Translated by Richard Philcox. New York: Grove Press.

Sekyi-Otu, Ato (1996). *Fanon's Dialectic of Experience*. Cambridge, MA: Harvard University Press.

Sekyi-Otu, Ato (2003). 'Fanon and the Possibility of Postcolonial Critical Imagination'. Council for the Development of Social Science Research in Africa Symposium on Canonical Works and Continuing Innovations in African Arts and Humanities. University of Ghana, Legon, Accra, 17–19 September.

Spivak, Gayatri Chakravorty (1999). *A Critique of Postcolonial Reason: Toward a History of the Vanishing Present*. Cambridge, Mass: Harvard University Press.

Vázquez-Arroyo, Antonio Y. (2018). 'Decolonial feints: Ciccariello-Maher's *Decolonizing Dialectics*'. *Theory and Event* 21(1): 324–29.

Young, Robert (1990). *White Mythologies: Writing History and the West*. London and New York: Routledge.

Contributors

Robert Bernasconi is Edwin Erle Sparks Professor of Philosophy and African American Studies at Pennsylvania State University. He is the author of two books on Heidegger and of *How to Read Sartre*, as well as numerous articles on the critical philosophy of race and continental philosophy. He is the editor of three journals: *Critical Philosophy of Race*, *Levinas Studies* and *Eco-Ethica*.

Ulrike Kistner is Professor in the Department of Philosophy at the University of Pretoria. Her research and teaching are focused on political philosophy, social theory, aesthetic theory and psychoanalytic theory. She is the translator of the first edition of Freud's *Three Essays on the Theory of Sexuality* (Verso, [1905] 2016).

Reingard Nethersole is Professor Emerita at the University of the Witwatersrand, where she established the Department of Comparative Literature in 1978 and served as its first chair for ten years. She has authored some eighty scholarly articles on literary theory and continental philosophy. She is a visiting lecturer at the University of Richmond, Virginia, where she has taught topics in global literatures and postcolonialism.

Ato Sekyi-Otu is Professor Emeritus in the Department of Social Science and the Graduate Programme in Social and Political Thought at York University, Toronto. He is an Associate Fellow of Thinking Africa in the Department of Political and International Studies, Rhodes University, Grahamstown. He taught courses in social and political thought at York University from 1971 to 2006, and is the author of *Fanon's Dialectic of Experience* (Harvard University Press, 1996) and *Left Universalism, Africacentric Essays* (Routledge, 2018).

Beata Stawarska is Professor of Philosophy at the University of Oregon. She is the author of *Saussure's Philosophy of Language as Phenomenology* (Oxford University Press, 2015) and *Between You and I: Dialogical Phenomenology* (Ohio University Press, 2009), as well as several essays in contemporary European philosophy. She is an expert in the fields of phenomenology, structuralism and poststructuralism, and feminism, and is currently at work on a project on martial morality and the ambiguity of violence.

Josias Tembo is a doctoral researcher at the Center for Contemporary European Philosophy at Radboud University in Nijmegen, and a research associate in the Department of Philosophy at the University of Pretoria. His research is in the field of political philosophy, with a focus on the philosophy of race and African philosophy. His doctoral research is on the constellation of race and religion in conceptions of political belonging.

Philippe Van Haute is Professor of Philosophical Anthropology at Radboud University, Nijmegen, and Extraordinary Professor at the University of Pretoria. He is a psychoanalyst of the Belgian School of Psychoanalysis, of which he was president from 2006 to 2009. He has published several books and numerous articles on the relation between philosophy and psychoanalysis, including (with Tomas Geyskens) *A Non-Oedipal Psychoanalysis? Clinical Anthropology of Hysteria in the Works Freud and Lacan* (Louvain University Press, 2012) and (with Herman Westerink) *Reading Freud's Three Essays on the Theory of Sexuality: Pleasure, Sexuality and the Object* (Routledge, forthcoming).

Index

Printed and bound by CPI Group (UK) Ltd, Croydon, CR0 4YY

13/04/2025

14656575-0003